The Soweto Uprising

OHIO SHORT HISTORIES OF AFRICA

This series of Ohio Short Histories of Africa is meant for those who are looking for a brief but lively introduction to a wide range of topics in African history, politics, and biography, written by some of the leading experts in their fields.

The Soweto Uprising

Noor Nieftagodien

OHIO UNIVERSITY PRESS

ATHENS, OHIO

Ohio University Press, Athens, Ohio 45701
www.ohioswallow.com

First published by Jacana Media (Pty) Ltd in 2014
10 Orange Street
Sunnyside
Auckland Park 2092
South Africa
+27 011 628 3200
www.jacana.co.za

To obtain permission to quote, reprint, or otherwise reproduce
or distribute material from Ohio University Press publications,
please contact our rights and permissions department at (740)
593-1154 or (740) 593-4536 (fax).

First published in North America in 2015 by Ohio University Press
Printed in the United States of America
Ohio University Press books are printed on acid-free paper ⊗ ™

ISBN: 978-0-8214-2154-3
e-ISBN: 978-0-8214-4523-5

Library of Congress Cataloging-in-Publication Data available

Cover design by Joey Hi-Fi

Contents

1

Causes and character

The student uprising of 16 June 1976 marked a decisive turning point in South Africa's history. Together with the Durban strikes of 1973, it marked the end of the political quiescence that fell over South Africa in the wake of the Sharpeville massacre and inaugurated a reawakening of black resistance, which ultimately brought apartheid to its knees. On that historic day thousands of Soweto's students marched behind a single demand – 'Away with Afrikaans!' Undoubtedly the immediate cause of the uprising was the state's decision to impose Afrikaans as a medium of instruction in urban African schools. Students interpreted the policy as part of the government's ideological assault with the intention of undermining black education yet further and entrenching the secondary status of black youth.

Helena Pohlandt-McCormick has argued that the imposition of Afrikaans 'was an assertion of power whose structures and ideology would disempower and create perpetual minors of Africans'. Buoyed by apartheid's success in the 1960s, the National Party became imbued

7

with ideological arrogance, imagining it could impose its doctrinaire racist agenda on the black population with impunity. But, contrary to its intentions, 'Afrikaans became the symbol of the state's illegitimacy'. It was evident in the months before and subsequent to the historic march that the struggle against Afrikaans was not simply a problem about language. Encapsulated in the rejection of Afrikaans was a series of grievances about Bantu Education, the dire conditions in the townships, the suppression of black discontent and the denial of black aspirations. In other words, the system – apartheid – had become unbearable.

Despite growing dissatisfaction among black people, political mobilisation remained very limited in the townships during the late 1960s and early 1970s. But there were two parallel processes unfolding in this period that would converge and fundamentally alter black politics. Firstly, there was a sharp increase in the number of African students, especially in secondary schools. For the first time in the country's history there were millions of black students at school, constituting an important social force. Secondly, Black Consciousness provided young black students with the political tools to understand the nature of their oppression and inculcated in them a spirit of defiance. It also provided political cohesion to what was initially fragmented and dispersed resistance and it openly challenged white hegemony. Black Consciousness had been developed by Steve Biko and his comrades at tertiary institutions, where it quickly gained widespread support. While black university students were to the fore in openly defying white minority rule, their small numbers nationally limited the broader impact of their action. By contrast, the significantly larger school student population possessed much greater potential to influence resistance politics. The 1976 uprising was characterised by the autonomous action of black school students, who mobilised on their own, built their own independent organisations, and crafted political programmes and tactics in the face of severe state repression.

Crisis of apartheid

The 1960s represented the golden age of apartheid: black resistance had been crushed, government policies were implemented largely in accordance with the ideological imperatives of apartheid, the economy experienced unprecedented growth, white prosperity scaled new heights and the ruling National Party consolidated its grip on state power. From the late 1950s the government began introducing changes to key aspects of its policies, inaugurating the phase of 'high apartheid', which sought to consolidate white minority rule. A central aim was to reverse African urbanisation, to reduce the African presence in 'white' urban areas and to bolster the African population of the ethnic 'homelands'. The renewed emphasis on and politicisation of ethnicity were exemplified by the passing of the Promotion of

Bantu Self-Government Act in 1959, which signalled the government's intention to attach all Africans to a 'tribal' community and authority. At the same time Africans were denied a permanent status in the urban areas. 'Separate development' became the principal ideological tool used to legitimise the continued disenfranchisement of black people.

A leading government minister, M.C. Botha, expressed the state's policy in this way: 'natives without work or who, as approved workers, have misbehaved, must disappear out of white South Africa, back to the reserves'. Pass controls were also stepped up, which caused the number of pass convictions to increase from close to 380,000 to about 693,000 between 1963 and 1968. Consequently, the number of Africans residing in white urban areas decreased by approximately 200,000, while the population of the homelands increased by nearly one million.

Control over the black population was, of course, also achieved through political repression, specifically the prohibition of black political organisations and the implementation of coercive laws that resulted in the detention, long-term imprisonment, banning or banishment of 'troublesome' individuals, as well as killings by judicial and extra-judicial means. Once political stability and control were achieved, foreign and local investors renewed their support for apartheid, with capital inflows reaching new heights: between 1965 and

1974 more than R3500 million was invested in the local economy. In the 1960s South Africa's GDP increased by between 6 and 8 per cent a year (some suggest a figure of 9 per cent), making it one of the star performers of the global economy. Two noteworthy structural changes occurred at the time: a sharp increase in the monopolisation of the economy and a growth of capital-intensive production. Both processes created a demand for better-educated and skilled labour. While still dependent on and benefiting from relatively cheap labour, industrialists began to demand a steady supply of semi-skilled African labour, which would have far-reaching consequences for the state's education policy for Africans.

From the vantage of the late 1960s it must have appeared to the state, capital and the white population generally that the system of apartheid – of white power and privilege – was secure and unchallenged. However, even at the height of apartheid's success, there were already troubling signs on the horizon. A brief recession in 1968 was regarded as an aberration at the time, especially as the economy recovered reasonably quickly and positive growth ensued for a few years thereafter, albeit not at the same levels as before. But this apparent economic hiccup proved to be a harbinger of a much deeper crisis. In retrospect, the period from the late 1960s to the mid-1970s could be viewed as a transition from stability to structural crisis affecting every aspect of society. As the multi-faceted crisis unfolded, contestations arose between different factions in the state and between the state and capital over crucial policy issues, relating particularly to the position of black labour in the industrial economy. The most important manifestation of the emerging crisis was the reawakening of black protest, dramatically represented by the 1973 Durban workers' strikes and the 1976 students' uprising.

As the economy slipped into crisis, the position of black workers came under serious threat. By the mid-1970s the local economy was in the midst of a full-scale recession. As Dan O'Meara has shown, manufacturing output experienced a sharp decline of 6 per cent in the year 1974/75. Worse was to come the following year, when almost every sector of the industrial economy registered steep declines in production. The national economy stagnated in 1976 (showing 0 per cent growth) and over the next decade it grew at a pedestrian rate of only 1.9 per cent. With profit levels under pressure, foreign investment declined, while capital outflows accelerated: as a result, total investment fell precipitously by 13 per cent between 1975 and 1977. One crucial consequence of the economic crisis was a sharp rise in unemployment, especially among African workers. In 1962 the number of unemployed Africans stood at 582,000 but increased to one million in 1970, and more than doubled to reach 2.3 million in 1976. The cost of items on which the working class spent most of its income – food, clothing and transport – increased by 40 per cent between 1958 and 1971 and then, in the financial year 1972/73, by a staggering 30 per cent. The economic crisis affected black workers most severely, and from the late 1960s they began to be more vocal in demanding higher wages.

In January 1973 about 2000 African workers at Coronation Brick and Tile Company in Durban went on strike for a minimum wage of R30 a week. Soon, other workers in the city joined them, and by the end of March more than 160 strikes (involving approximately 60,000 workers) were recorded, easily eclipsing the number of strikes for the entire 1960s. The 1973 strike wave in Durban sparked a resurgence in black trade unions and for the first time in more than a decade black workers exhibited the collective will to challenge white *baasskap* (dominance) on the factory floor. Within a few years independent unions were launched in the major industrial centres and engaged in protracted struggles with employers over recognition and wages and against arbitrary dismissals. This reassertion of black workers' militancy constituted the first part of the twin rebirth of black resistance. The second occurred in the townships and was led by students.

Demise of 'model' townships

From the mid-1950s the apartheid government systematically and often ruthlessly destroyed old locations, removing their residents to segregated 'group areas' and new townships. Hundreds of thousands of black people were dragooned into 'properly planned' or 'model' townships, which were designed to give expression to racial segregation and social control. Soweto was the exemplar of this process. It grew rapidly as a result of mass housing provision funded by the state and through a loan of R6 million from the Anglo American Corporation. In the decade from 1955 to 1965 approximately 4400 houses a year were built in Soweto. New areas such as Dlamini, Chiawelo, Emdeni, Phiri and Zola were created in this period, representing the most remarkable expansion of one township complex. It marked the emergence of Soweto as the largest African township in the country, with an estimated 87,500 houses in 1966. It was also the high point of housing provision for Africans living in urban areas in apartheid South Africa.

'Model' townships such as Soweto, Daveyton, Katlehong, KwaThema, Sebokeng and Atteridgeville were designed to maximise control over the African population. Their grid lay-out, controlled access points and mast-lights aimed to ensure effective state surveillance. White administration of townships was augmented with the creation of Bantu Administration Boards in the early 1970s, which gave the central government direct control over the management of township matters. In addition, the police force, comprising a handful of white police, assisted by an army of notorious 'blackjacks' (black municipal police), enforced apartheid's draconian policies in townships. There were 900 'blackjacks' in Soweto alone and they were particularly ruthless in policing pass laws. In 1976 approximately a quarter of a million African men and women were arrested on pass offences nationally.

The government's decision to promote the 'homelands' resulted in a massive reallocation of resources away from black urban areas to the Bantustans. Between 1968 and 1975 expenditure on African housing in urban areas plummeted by 80 per cent: in 1967/68 the state spent R14.4 million on African housing, but three years later that figure was nearly halved to R7.7 million and by 1976/77 stood at a paltry R2.2 million. Between 1966 and 1969 the state built fewer than 2000 new houses in the entire Soweto. By the early 1970s the extent of the mounting housing crisis in Soweto became apparent. In 1970s the township's official population figure was 597,390, although government statistics generally undercounted the real size of township populations. The Urban Foundation suggested that Soweto's population in the late 1970s was likely to be closer to one million.

The decline in the construction of houses and the attendant increase in population caused a severe housing shortage in most townships across the country. In the mid-1970s there were slightly more than 100,000 dwellings in Soweto, accommodating an officially estimated population of approximately 600,000. But an industry survey in 1970 found an average of 13 people living in each 'matchbox' house in the township. Five years later that figure had increased to 17. Moreover, only

14 per cent of households had electricity and a meagre 3 per cent had access to hot water.

Frustration and anger mounted among township residents over the decline in their living standards as well as the state's tight grip on their everyday lives. But the repression of the 1960s continued to hold the lid down on the boiling pot and the absence of organisations stymied the emergence of a concerted political response to the growing list of grievances. When the government decided to impose Afrikaans as a medium of instruction in schools, it inadvertently provided a central focus around which opposition to Bantu Education and the whole system of apartheid could coalesce.

Bantu Education

The state's language policy, particularly the use of Afrikaans as a medium of instruction in African schools, was an important pillar in the edifice of Bantu Education. Implemented in the early 1950s, Bantu Education was designed to keep African people permanently subjected at the lower levels of society. H.F. Verwoerd, the so-called architect of apartheid, explained the underlying objective of the system as follows: 'There is no place for him [the Bantu] in the European community above the level of certain forms of labour.' Bantu Education was therefore central to the maintenance of a racially segregated system and part of the state's broader strategy to bring Africans under control. 'The education system',

Jonathan Hyslop has argued, 'was harnessed to the implementation of apartheid policy. In pursuit of the Nationalist government's aim of uprooting the urban African working class, the development of secondary, technical and higher education for Africans in the urban areas was strangled, so as to drive young people to seek their educational future in the Bantustans.'

Besides being significantly inferior to the education provided for the white population, the problems attending Bantu Education were aggravated in Soweto in the 1960s when the state stopped building more schools. At the same time, between 1955 and 1969 the number of African pupils increased from about 1 million to 2.5 million, causing overcrowding to become endemic. The average pupil–teacher ratio grew to 58:1 in 1967 from an already high 46:1 at the time the system was introduced. The quality of education was also severely undermined by the large numbers of unqualified and underqualified teachers: between 1965 and 1976 the percentage of teachers in African secondary and high schools with university degrees hovered between 1.4% and 2.5%. Not surprisingly, the students suffered as a result; this was reflected in the decline of the matric pass rate from 54 to 33 per cent between 1948 and 1968. Despite these appalling conditions in township schools, Bantu Education did not face significant student challenges during the 1960s.

From the early 1970s, however, important changes began to be introduced in African schooling that would have far-reaching consequences. At the time the government was under increasing pressure from industrialists to respond to the dire lack of skilled African workers. Eventually the government decided to make central funds available for the construction of schools in urban townships, which opened the way for a massive expansion of African schooling. High school enrolment as a percentage of total enrolment among African students increased modestly from 3.5 to 4.5 per cent between 1955 and 1970. From 1965 to 1970 the number of African students in secondary schools registered reasonably steep increases, from 66,906 to 122,489. Over the next five years, that figure jumped to 318,568.

Despite 40 new schools being built in Soweto in the early 1970s, the rapid growth in student numbers aggravated overcrowding. But in response to the deepening economic crisis of the early 1970s, the state again drastically reduced its spending on African education. The problem was compounded by amendments to the structure of African schooling. The eight-year primary and five-year secondary model was abandoned in favour of an even split of six years of primary and six years of secondary. The new system was introduced at the beginning of 1976, which meant that all those who had passed Std 5 and Std 6 in 1975 would leave primary school, resulting in a massive bulge in the first year of secondary school.

Students: new force of change

A crucial consequence of these rapid changes in schooling in the early 1970s was the creation of a large population of African students. In 1976, there were 3.7 million young Africans in schools, of whom 389,000 were in secondary institutions. Across the country students faced similar experiences of overcrowding, poor teaching, and dismal prospects. The common awareness of the problems with Bantu Education was felt most profoundly in the urban townships, which had a high concentration of schools. In Soweto alone, the number of students nearly doubled from 90,000 at the end of the 1960s to 170,000 in 1976. In the brief period between 1972 and 1974, the number of secondary school students increased from 12,656 to 34,656. African students now constituted a significant social force, whose size was unparalleled in the country's history. Ironically, Bantu Education had created its own gravediggers.

Inspired by Black Consciousness, students in Soweto began to turn to resistance politics well before June 1976. Initially their efforts were fragmented, small-scale and often ephemeral. Slowly but ineluctably a new cadre of young activists took shape. Groups of classmates, clusters of street friends, team mates in soccer clubs, members of debating societies or of cultural and religious groups began to engage in rudimentary resistance politics. This mainly took the form of reading radical literature, discussions and debates. Over time some of these groups

19

became overtly political, while increasing contact (especially at schools) helped create informal networks of activists.

It was out of this process that the leadership of the Soweto uprising emerged. Students independently organised and led the struggles in each of the three major phases of the Soweto rebellion of 1976–7. In the first half of 1976 schools directly affected by the introduction of Afrikaans, mainly the junior secondary schools, mounted local demonstrations without support from existing student political organisations. The second phase, the uprising of June, was led by an Action Committee, comprising mostly political activists from SASM, who tended to be high school students. During the final phase, which commenced in August, the Soweto Students' Representative Council led the mobilisation of students and the broader township community. In this movement, adults and established political organisations, both internal and external, were largely peripheral actors.

Narratives and claims of ownership
For many years after the eruption in 1976, two major narratives existed about the student uprising. At the time the apartheid government attempted to portray the students as a uniform mass of unruly and undisciplined militants. In its view, the students' reaction to the new language policy was uninformed and irrational. The Cillie Commission of Inquiry, established by the government

to investigate the 'disturbances' of 1976, unsurprisingly came to similar conclusions. It absolved the state, especially the police, of responsibility for the violence and accused students of instigating attacks on the police, whites and government property without good cause. Few people outside the laager of apartheid's supporters gave any credence to this official narrative.

A second narrative, produced by the ANC, has attempted to claim ownership of the student uprising. Soon after the uprising, a leading ANC member, Alfred Nzo, averred: 'some of these youths are long standing members of our Organisation who, consistent with revolutionary commitment of all members of our movement to the cause of our people, have actively participated from the beginning of the uprising, giving whatever leadership was possible under the exceptionally difficult circumstances.' Especially since 1994, the ANC has actively produced a narrative promoting its leading position in the liberation struggle. In doing so, it has appropriated key events in that struggle for its own history. The Sharpeville massacre, the Soweto student rebellion and countless factory and township uprisings have been inserted as signposts on the ANC's supposedly inevitable march to becoming the government of liberation. Constructing this dominant narrative of liberation history has involved the marginalisation of other actors, including other national liberation movements (for example, the Pan Africanist Congress and the Black Consciousness Movement), many local organisations and independent trade unions. Most importantly, as Gary Baines has argued in relation to the Soweto uprising, the agency of students has been airbrushed out in order to conform to an ANC-centric liberation history. In her perceptive study of the student rebellion, Pohlandt-McCormick argues that despite the fundamental incompatibility between the discourses of the apartheid government and of the ANC, both 'tended to disregard or silence participants' voices and de-emphasise their conscious will, agency and reason'.

Perhaps the most frank reflection of the ANC's capacity at the time was offered by its president in exile, O.R. Tambo. On the tenth anniversary of the rebellion, Tambo wrote: 'Organisationally, in political and military terms, we were too weak to take advantage of the situation that crystallised from the first events of 16 June 1976. We had very few active ANC units inside the country. We had no military presence so to speak of. The communication links between ourselves outside the country and the masses of our people were still too slow and weak to meet the situation such as was posed by the Soweto uprising.' Although the ANC was the main beneficiary of the movement of large numbers of black youth into exile, it did not play a significant role in the uprising itself.

Oral history and counter-narratives
In the aftermath of the uprising, scholars from diverse intellectual and ideological backgrounds sought to

analyse the causes, character and consequences of the student movement. Baruch Hirson's *Year of Fire, Year of Ash. The Soweto Revolt: Roots of a Revolution?* was a seminal radical analysis, while John Kane-Berman's *Soweto: Black Revolt – White Reaction* became the standard liberal text on the historic events. In the pages of the journal *Review of African Political Economy*, the veteran intellectuals Ruth First and Archie Mafeje crossed swords with their different interpretation of the character of the youth uprising and its relationship to the broader class and national struggle. Largely missing from these analyses were the voices of the principal participants, the students.

From the mid-1990s there developed a new generation of studies that sought to place the voices, experiences and interpretations of students at the centre of new narratives. Among the most influential of these texts are Sifiso Ndlovu's *The Soweto Uprising: Counter-Memories of June 1976*; Helena Pohlandt-McCormick's doctoral thesis, '"I Saw a Nightmare …" Doing Violence to Memory: The Soweto Uprising, June 16, 1976'; Sibongile Mkhabela's *Open Earth and Black Roses: Remembering 16 June 1976*; Philip Bonner and Lauren Segal's *Soweto: A History*; the contributions in Ali Hlongwane's edited collection, *Footprints of the 'Class of 76': Commemoration, Memory, Mapping and Heritage*; and *Soweto 16 June 1976: Personal Accounts of the Uprising*, compiled by Elsabe Brink, Steve Lebelo, Sue Krige and Dumisane Ntshangase. A salient feature of this diverse body of work is the reliance on oral testimonies from participants – both leaders and rank-and-file members of the student movement. Ndlovu and Mkhabela were participants themselves, and Mkhabela the most senior female student leader. Participants' voices and views have of course always been present and available, but were mostly omitted in published texts. Collectively, the works I have listed have produced multiple narratives, new insights and critical interpretations of the June uprising. In the process they have also generated counter-narratives to the versions produced by those in power. This pocketbook relies heavily on the oral testimonies and varied interpretations published in these texts.

Foregrounding the multiple voices of students has contributed to the development of new interpretations, which not only demonstrate the autonomy of students and their organisations, but also highlight their courage and political innovation. The student movement was diverse and complex. High school and junior school students were not initially united; divergent political views vied for supremacy; and student organisations were generally weak. Nonetheless, the movement achieved a remarkable degree of unity. Male and female students marched and died together. Although the leadership of the movement was dominated by young men, their female counterparts were active throughout, in meetings, on the streets and in detention. Students had to navigate all manner of political difficulties and their inexperience inevitably resulted in wrong turns and poor judgements. However, at the same time they demonstrated great political acuity in the face of state repression and scepticism from adults. By drawing on the rich archive of oral histories of the Soweto uprising, this book provides an interpretation of those historic events that places the myriad experiences of students at the centre and explains how they not only inaugurated a township revolution but also reconfigured black resistance politics in South Africa.

2

Political reawakening in Soweto

There is now an established and well-rehearsed
narrative of the evolution of resistance politics in the
post-Sharpeville era. According to this, state repression
ushered in a period of relative political quiescence until
the early 1970s, when the Durban strikes of 1973 and the
student rebellion of 1976 signalled the reawakening of the
anti-apartheid struggle. Scholars have given considerable
attention to the re-emergence of the independent trade
union movement, the 1976 uprising and, to a lesser
extent, the birth and growth of the Black Consciousness
Movement.

However, there remains a dearth of research on the
subterranean activities that went into the rebuilding
of the resistance movements in townships during this
period. It is a neglect that is arguably due to several
interrelated factors. First, histories of resistance tend to
be preoccupied with major events or moments of high
contestation between contending forces. Second, the
notion of politically autonomous movements emerging
in the early 1970s deviates from the hegemonic narrative

National Archives of South Africa

constructed since the early 1990s in which this period is presented as a mere hiatus in the linear progression of the ANC from dominant liberation movement to ruling party. Consequently, there continues to be a lack of interest in engaging the low-level and inchoate politics of dissent during the interregnum between Sharpeville and the big moments of the early and mid-1970s. To be fair, there have been efforts recently to account for the 'sounds in the silence' of the 1960s, but these have generally focused on the activities of either the armed wings of the liberation movements or above-ground (legal) organisations such as the National Union of South African Students (NUSAS).

One way of reimagining this period is to view the year 1969 as the beginning of the reconfiguration of resistance politics. Indeed, it was an important year in the history of the anti-apartheid struggle: Steve Biko and his comrades established the South African Students' Organisation (SASO), migrant dockworkers went on strike for higher wages in Durban, and the ANC held an important strategic conference in Morogoro, Tanzania. It may appear counter-intuitive to regard these events as harbingers of future resistance, if one considers the contemporary power and stability of the apartheid state. However, within a few years Black Consciousness had established itself as the primary ideology of resistance among young black people in the country and inspired a proliferation of local organisations. In 1973 thousands of workers in Durban went on strike to demand higher wages, thereby setting in train the rebuilding of the independent black trade union movement. By contrast, the ANC's presence in the country remained quite weak and it was not able to exert any serious influence on black politics during these years. What this shift of focus permits is an inquiry into the nascent movements of resistance that emerged in townships and education institutions during a period of repression and in circumstances where the historic liberation organisations were too weak and far removed to orchestrate the myriad activities that constituted the political renaissance. These new movements profoundly shaped the character of the student uprising in 1976.

The political reawakening of black South Africans from the late 1960s also marked their re-entry into the broader anti-colonial struggles that had been sweeping across the African continent during that decade. In particular, the collapse of Portuguese colonialism and the subsequent attainment of independence by Mozambique and Angola engendered enormous excitement among black youths. It seemed that the demise of the last colonial outposts in southern Africa (Rhodesia, South West Africa and South Africa) was just a matter of time. The Black Consciousness Movement organised 'Viva Frelimo' rallies to celebrate the coming to power of a radical movement in Mozambique.

As we have seen, the process of political rejuvenation developed along two parallel tracks: the workplace and the township. In this book the focus is on the townships (principally Soweto), where the emerging movements were mostly distinguished by their youthful character. Young people who became politically active at the time had very little direct experience of the mass movements of the 1950s when the ANC and the PAC made their mark as the leading liberation organisations. Consequently, there was no prior allegiance to these bodies among the young activists, who, in the first instance, created their own home-grown movements. Only later, particularly in the aftermath of the 1976 uprising, were more substantive connections forged between significant sections of the new generation of youth activists and the exile organisations.

It was also a period of political fluidity and experimentation, which resonated with experiences in other parts of the world where resistance politics were being reconstituted in circumstances of repression. Young black people were inspired by a whole range of ideas and experiences emanating from global struggles against oppression. They exhibited an insatiable thirst for political knowledge, manifested by the circulation of an eclectic body of radical literature. Books and pamphlets on Marxism, anti-colonial struggles and the civil rights campaigns in the United States were widely read and debated. Works by anti-colonial intellectuals such as Frantz Fanon and Kwame Nkrumah were popular, as were speeches and writings by Malcolm X, Martin Luther King and Mao Zedong. Initially, universities were at the centre of this new wave of political education, but high school students were also increasingly drawn into similar activities of conscientisation.

This political rebirth consisted of various strands, which tended to be disparate, small-scale and initially disconnected. In the formative years of rebuilding, groups often coalesced around friendship or school-based networks. In conditions of repression, familiarity and trust were critical ingredients in the embryonic stages of constituting rudimentary political units. Over time these local groups connected to similar units, thus developing networks of like-minded activists across geographical boundaries. One informant captures the growing political awareness and inexperience prevalent at the time: 'We were, of course, very alive to the fact that we as black people were being oppressed. The students especially were quite sensitive to this and we were all the time trying to find a way of doing something about it. It was just unfortunate that we were not so clear about how to show our anger and resentment in a clear political way. But we certainly expressed ourselves indirectly in things like poetry reading and so on.'

Some of the groups that were established focused on addressing local issues, such as the authoritarian behaviour of school principals or teachers and the absence of social facilities in the townships. Many of them were therefore not explicitly political at the beginning but invariably were transformed over a short period of time into spaces of political education and activism. There were also a few groups that consciously aimed to become part of the armed struggle and deliberately set out to establish contact with either the ANC or PAC. What all this demonstrates is an organic process of generating a new cohort of politically aware youth who became involved in the slow and painstaking work of laying the foundation of political movements in the townships, corresponding to a similar process under way in workplaces. Most of these youth-led political activities were either inspired by or directly initiated by the Black Consciousness Movement.

Black Consciousness

SASO's launch at the University of the North (Turfloop) in July 1969 was a turning point in the history of black student organisations. Under Steve Biko's leadership, the new movement spent the next few years formulating a set of ideas that would constitute the essence of Black Consciousness. In 1971 SASO issued a policy manifesto in which it declared its main aim as being the liberation of 'the black man, first from psychological oppression' and secondly from 'physical oppression'. Black people were defined as those who were 'politically, economically and socially discriminated against as a group in South African society and identifying themselves as a unit in the struggle towards the realisation of their aspirations'. 'The Black Man', SASO asserted, 'must build up his own value system, see himself as self-defined and not defined by others.' Leaders of the Black Consciousness Movement launched powerful critiques of Bantu Education, Bantustans and white minority rule in general. The militant tone of these criticisms was novel and inspirational for a generation accustomed to the muted dissent expressed by older people. SASO produced its own publication, *SASO News*, which was edited by Steve Biko. At its peak, thousands of copies were distributed nationally among students. The radical ideas and sense of defiance espoused by the Black Consciousness Movement struck a powerful chord among large sections of black youth, especially in schools and universities.

This spirit of defiance was most memorably demonstrated in April 1972 at the University of the North when the popular student leader and president of the local Students' Representative Council, Onkgopotse Tiro, was asked to address a ceremony of new graduates. He used the opportunity to deliver a stinging critique of the white administration of black universities and of Bantu Education to a packed hall of black students, with the university's white administrators in attendance. His expulsion a few days later hardly came as a surprise, but it triggered a mass walk-out by students, who demanded his reinstatement. In May, other black universities joined the boycott in a show of solidarity. Although Tiro was not reinstated, his brazen challenge to white authority reflected a sea-change in the politics of black students. In 1972 students at the University of the Western Cape protested against the preponderance of white staff and regular police raids against SASO, and in reaction the institution was closed. Struggles also took place at the University of Durban-Westville.

Two important consequences followed from these events. If they had not done so already, black students – those classified as African, coloured and Indian – now embraced Black Consciousness, asserting a united black identity against white minority rule. Furthermore, the closure of universities by white authorities created opportunities for this newly politicised cohort of students to use the time to embark on programmes of conscientisation in their home communities. By the early 1970s, the ideas of Black Consciousness had spread across the country, however unevenly. In 1972 SASO could claim a membership of between 4000 and 6000.

In the same year the SASO leadership was instrumental in convening the Black People's Convention (BPC). Held in December 1972 in the peri-urban township of Hammanskraal, outside Pretoria, the BPC was an initiative that aimed to extend and consolidate the organisational reach of Black Consciousness beyond its initial base of the universities. Attended by an impressive 1400 delegates representing about 145 student, religious and community bodies, the conference reflected the growing popularity of Black Consciousness. There was also a clear commitment to translating support for the ideas of the movement into vibrant organisations. The BPC itself resolved to 'To preach, popularise and implement the philosophy of Black Consciousness'.

Until 1972 the apartheid state appeared mildly tolerant of the emergence of SASO and the Black Consciousness Movement in general. However, public displays of defiance and the obvious popularity of the militancy advocated by members of the movement soon made the authorities aware of the potential challenge Black Consciousness could pose to the system. As a result, the state moved to quash the new movement by attempting to silence its leadership. In 1973 it banned several leaders of SASO and BPC. Steve Biko, Bokwe Mafuna, Barney Pityana, Jerry Modisane, Harry Nengwekhulu and Saths Cooper had severe restrictions imposed on them. This obviously had an adverse effect on the Black Consciousness Movement, causing its constitutive organisations to experience uneven success in establishing themselves across the country. However, an assessment of the political influence of Black Consciousness cannot be reduced to its organisational base. Of arguably greater importance was its impact in the realm of ideas and its capacity to inspire various sections of black society well beyond its formal reach.

The 1970s has been seen as a period of 'cultural renaissance', profoundly affected by Black Consciousness. Poetry, music, art, theatre and literature all flourished as a new desire for 'self-definition' and 'self-actualisation' took root in black society. This black cultural renaissance, suffused with ideas drawn from Black Consciousness, was particularly evident in the burgeoning form of protest theatre. Uncle Tom's Hall in Orlando West was a mecca of this cultural revolution. Patrick Sekuthi, who was at high school in the early 1970s, remembers that 'around that period you know there were plays, so we used to go there to watch those, they stimulated us you know'. *Sizwe Banzi Is Dead*, Fugard's iconic play with John Kani in the lead, resonated with the anger felt by a growing number of black youth. Sekuthi captures the power of the play: 'We were already political-minded and when we were exposed to such plays, where we could see this gentleman acting a part of a father who is being harassed by a teenager white police boy harassing him and then taking off his hat and squeezing that hat. And when you know at home when your dad comes in he takes off the hat he holds that hat, tidily and so on, it's your dad's hat ... from work. You feel proud about your dad and you are the one who has to put that hat safely somewhere and now it's been crackly squeezed and that. Now he was holding an orange, in symbolising a hat, and then squeezing that orange. You know it affected us, it touched us and that really, now that on its own conscientised us and then made us aware ... a black man's life really is worthless.'

A similar convergence developed between religious organisations and Black Consciousness, especially among the youth and others who became drawn to liberation theology. The University Christian Movement (UCM) and the Student Christian Movement (SCM) served as spaces of political apprenticeship for many activists who later became prominent figures in political organisations. In many cases, there was a significant overlap between the membership of these religious formations and political movements.

At the same time Black Consciousness began to attract a growing number of adherents among high-school students, particularly in Soweto. Young and newly qualified teachers, who had been exposed to the politics of Black Consciousness at tertiary institutions, entered the profession exactly at a time when there was a massive expansion of township high schools. One of the reasons given by many high-school activists for the spread of Black Consciousness ideas was the influence of progressive young teachers, several of whom taught history. Onkgopotse Tiro was perhaps the most well known of these teacher activists. His expulsion from Turfloop brought Tiro to the attention of the security police, which made it difficult for him to enrol at other educational institutions or to find work. Fortunately, the sympathetic principal at Morris Isaacson, Mr Lekgau Mathabathe, employed him as a part-time history teacher in early 1973. Although Tiro was removed within six months, his brief stint at the school is remembered as a key moment in the political awakening of many of his students. Other young teachers followed in his footsteps. Sydney Ramokgopa and his fellow comrades who were at Morris Isaacson in the early 1970s remember the history teacher Ralph Manyane and the SASO members Ralph Mothiba and a Mr Masiza, who introduced 'topics that really involve[d] the lives and the society in general'. These young Black Consciousness activists exposed students to an alternative education, mainly comprising African history and histories of black resistance, which served both as an explicit rejection of the official syllabus and as a political education.

Tiro's involvement in the political education of high-school students was cut short when, under threat of detention, he decided to skip the country and go into exile in Botswana. Here he continued mobilising support for the Black Consciousness Movement, became involved in international solidarity and sought to create unity between the different liberation movements. The security police still perceived him as a threat and on 1 February 1974 assassinated him, by means of a parcel-bomb. Tiro's death at the hands of the apartheid state made him a martyr in the eyes of students and young political activists. Previously, the killing of leading political activists might have struck fear into the hearts of many. Tiro's death, however, was met with anger and inspired many to follow his example of defiance and commitment. The students whom he influenced became important agents in transforming Soweto into a hub of youth and student dissent.

Early activist networks

The early 1970s was a time of political exploration, of searching for radical ideologies, developing critiques of apartheid and capitalism, and trying to work out how to overcome the system. It was an exciting time as young people began rebuilding the internal liberation movement, step by step. All over Soweto young activists were busy forming small groups – discussion circles, reading groups, debating societies – to grapple with radical ideologies and discover how best to organise themselves. A number of these groups operated in Orlando and involved students from the secondary schools. Patrick Sekuthi explains how concerns among some friends about the undemocratic appointment of prefects led to the formation of one such group: 'We sat together with Willy Nkonyela and

Raymond Pilane, then just debating topics that guys we need to do something about the system here at school. We are not so much happy about the way things are, eh it means that the administration of the school is forcing these prefects on us, now we need to chase this system, move away from where prefects would be chosen by the administration, we as students we should be in a position to choose our own prefects. So we roped in Sydney Ramokgopa, then we roped in Oupa Motlana ... we started now having meetings.'

However, before they could proceed, the principal got wind of the fact that they were meeting regularly. 'I don't know how this ended up in the principal's office, it came to his ear that these guys this is their intention, they normally hold meetings you know, when we are supposed to be in class, so they got to change the system so the police were called so they suspended us. Then he said if you want to come back you must bring along your parents.' The principal of Morris Isaacson at the time was Mr Mathabathe, who was evidently nervous about what appeared to be signs of political mobilisation at his school. But if Sekuthi and his comrades expected any sympathy from their parents they were mistaken. When he arrived with his mother, Mr Mathabathe reiterated the administration's policy regarding the appointment of prefects and told them that elections by students only happened at universities. He then gave them an ultimatum: if the students did not agree, they should go home with their parents – 'or go try their luck somewhere else'. Sekuthi's mother's response echoed the views of the other parents. 'So well my mom said, "Now look, Mr Mathabathe, this is my son and then as soon as he leaves this gate he stops to be my son, as soon as he reaches Morris Isaacson school gates and he enters those gates, that is your son, when he moves out from those gates he stops being my son and he ends up being your own son, so he's your responsibility."'

Mrs Sekuthi's intervention exposed an important and deep cleavage between youth and their parents. As Thami Zitha comments, 'during the 1960s our parents were afraid to talk about politics, because if they did they were going to be arrested … People did not trust each other.' Ramokgopa has a more critical opinion. In his view, 'our parents they were mostly very conservative'. 'I remember one time,' he says. 'We met one old man there, and this old man he said: "you will end up just like", he even said, "just like that fool Mothopeng [the later PAC leader]." Mothopeng was speaking openly, he didn't fear anything. So most of the parents they were really conservative, they didn't want that type of what Zephania Mothopeng was in. And they will always want to watch their children what they are doing.'

Ramokgopa came from a political family. Both his parents were aligned to the ANC in the 1950s and his father was probably a member of the organisation. His older brother was also an ANC member and went into exile in 1963, which resulted in regular harassment of the family by the security police. Perhaps because of this direct experience of the security forces, Ramokgopa's parents were nervous about the prospect of their young son also becoming involved in anti-apartheid politics. He believes that 'The politics of that old generation is that they were not open. Now the new generation it was open, and we saw what was happening. Like for instance when you look at the statement that Tiro made during the convocation in Turfloop, he was very open and clear. So really our parents during that time, there was, let us say, that fear of the system.'

Students and youth organisations take shape

In the early 1970s the growing political awareness among students and youth was manifested in the birth of new organisations. The two most significant bodies to emerge were the South African Students Movement (SASM) and the National Youth Organisation (NAYO). The first attempt to build an organisation among high-school students in Soweto occurred in either 1968 or 1970 with the establishment of the African Students' Movement (ASM). While there are differences of opinion about its founding date, what is not in dispute is that senior students from high schools in Orlando and Diepkloof were instrumental in its formation. For the historian Nozipho Diseko, the launch date of 1968 is important because it proves that ASM was created before SASO and thus independent of the Black Consciousness Movement. She also argues that neither the ANC nor the PAC had anything to do with ASM's formation. Her main claim seems to be that ASM comprised different political views and was not under the sway of any one ideology, especially not Black Consciousness. Nonetheless, at its origins ASM espoused an Africanist view, with its founders grappling with 'what it meant to be African'. According to Diseko, ASM was involved in three campaigns, namely, calling for the establishment of an SRC, the organisation of winter and summer schools, and a campaign against inter-school music competitions, which it claimed interfered with the formal curriculum.

By 1972 ASM had extended its presence to the following high schools: Orlando, Diepkloof, Morris Isaacson, Orlando West, Sekano Ntoane and Meadowlands. It is difficult to ascertain the organisational strength of ASM, but its support was very likely confined to a handful of activists. In 1972 SASO resolved to support the creation of a national student organisation, and called on ASM to act as one of the main vehicles to achieve this objective. The leaders of SASO and ASM quickly agreed on the need to unite all black high-school students across the country, and as a result SASM was launched in March 1973.

Over the following three years the new movement was subject to continuous police surveillance and harassment. In fact, as early as September 1973, SASM's first elected secretary, Mathe Diseko, was banned. This caused the fledgling movement considerable distress. SASM limped ahead but its aspiration to become a vibrant national movement had been dealt a serious blow. As a result, SASM remained mostly confined to Soweto, with pockets of support in other Rand townships. In June 1974 the BPC and SASO convened a meeting with SASM with the aim of rejuvenating the movement, and in September a new executive committee was elected, consisting of Doctor Moloto (president), Zwelinzima Sizani (vice-president), Nkosiyakhe Amos Masondo (secretary), Billy Masetlha (organiser) and Murphy Morobe (treasurer).

Efforts to strengthen the national organisation and to expand its geographical influence continued to register uneven success. Nonetheless, it was able to articulate the outlines of a political programme that echoed the ideas of the BCM: community projects, 'liberation of the black man', black awareness and solidarity. A proposed national action programme developed in 1975 focused mainly on education and on generating political awareness among students. A new executive was elected in that year: Vusi Tshabalala (president), Zuzile Cindi (vice-president), Billy Masetlha (general secretary) and Nkosiyakhe Masondo (organising secretary). However, the new executive soon suffered a double blow when Masondo was detained, while Cindi decided to go into exile in order to escape a similar fate. The high turnover of leadership proved debilitating and SASM was forced into survival mode, precisely at a time when Afrikaans began to appear as a

43

critical and contentious issue in Soweto's schools.

Elsewhere in townships in the Pretoria-Witwatersrand Vereeniging (PWV) area there was further evidence of high-school students becoming involved in opposition politics. For example, activists at Tembisa High in 1975 established the Tembisa Student Organisation. According to Mongezi Maphuthi, there was a discernible growth in support for Black Consciousness: 'As early as 1975 we started to be involved together with Sipho Mzolo in Alexandra, and others from the BC. I remember there was a commemoration for [Robert] Sobukwe in Alexandra, we went there. We did not have an ideology, we accepted everything that was brought by Black people.'

Obed Bapela remembers that SASM was active at the secondary school in Alexandra: 'The SASM people used to meet secretly ... they used to plan and discuss ... we [had] special classes where students will then group themselves and go into classrooms at the secondary school and study as a group ... Yet those sessions they used to double them up as studies but also as political discussions for their organisation SASM. So there was a branch of SASM very active but very underground type of structure where you will not just go and participate ordinarily.' SASM may have been organisationally weak, but its survival in the face of mounting repression was testimony to the commitment of its members. Moreover, it consisted of politically aware senior students, who commanded respect in the secondary and high schools.

This network of activists would become important in mobilising support for the struggles in 1976.

Many of the same activists also became involved in organising township youth who were not in educational institutions. In 1972, SASO members initiated the formation of the Natal Youth Organisation and Transvaal Youth Organisation. But as was often the case in this period, the constituent parts of these new co-ordinating structures were created through local activities. The founding of the Sharpeville Youth Club was a case in point. Established in 1972 as an informal network of friends, the Youth Club was formally launched in 1973. Among the founders were Vusi Tshabalala, Nkutshweu 'Skaap' Motsau and Leah Montsho. Their primary concern at the beginning was simply to keep the youth of Sharpeville active and out of mischief. Vusi Tshabalala recalls that they organised ballroom dancing, table tennis, drama, jazz sessions and poetry reading.

The Sharpeville Youth Club was another example of how a social club was quickly transformed into an explicitly political organisation in response to the emergence of broader oppositional politics. According to Tshabalala, members of the club were vaguely familiar with Black Consciousness and in late 1972 heard about a conference to be held in Hammanskraal. He and Motsau were sufficiently interested and collected money from family and friends to undertake the 170-kilometre journey. Arriving without an invitation, they were met with suspicion and were in danger of being sent packing. However, enough delegates believed they were genuinely interested and they were allowed to stay for the duration of the historic Black People's Convention. The two youngsters were enthralled by the political discussions and left the conference persuaded by the ideas of Black Consciousness. The following year they formalised the Sharpeville Youth Club, which then assisted in the opening of a Black People's Convention office in Vereeniging. Their politicisation was accelerated when the police arrested several members of the club. The subsequent trial of Motsau brought the group from Sharpeville to the attention of activists in Johannesburg's townships, who offered them solidarity.

As a result, Tshabalala and his comrades became involved in helping to unify the various local and provincial youth organisations. In July 1973 the Transvaal Youth Organisation, the Natal Youth Organisation and various smaller local organisations met to launch NAYO. Although the new youth organisation was independent of SASO and SASM, it was regarded as a critical component of the triumvirate of bodies in the stable of Black Consciousness that aimed to organise youth and student constituencies.

'Underground' defiance

Although the repression of the 1960s struck debilitating blows against the liberation movements, it did not completely destroy their support base in townships such as Soweto. Mass arrests and forced exile certainly removed many key leaders from the country or into prison and largely rendered established networks ineffective. Nonetheless, many of the activists who remained behind looked for opportunities to maintain rudimentary networks between themselves and also to connect with leadership structures in exile. Most of these efforts were necessarily clandestine and they all struggled to survive. An early example of efforts by a new generation of political activists to link up with an older generation occurred in the late 1960s and was centred on Orlando West and Diepkloof. A number of key activists who had been involved in the Congress Movement and especially the trade unions began to reach out to younger people with the aim of re-establishing some semblance of a political presence in the township. Winnie Mandela, Rita and Lawrence Nzanga, Samson Ndou and Joyce Sikhakhane were among those involved in this initiative. Snuki Zikalala, who lived in Diepkloof and attended school in Orlando, was drawn into this informal network by Winnie Mandela in 1966 or 1967. It is important to remember that this initiative was launched only two years after the conclusion of the Rivonia trial. George Mokwebo, Daniel Tsotetsi and Joseph Stimulo Banda were among other youths from Soweto who were recruited. Over the next few months the older activists attempted to provide these youths with basic political education.

'Joyce [Sikhakhane] gave us ANC politics. Then the second week we organised another meeting at my place. What she did she brought Samson Ndou. He also came and gave us a number of ANC politics. Then they started introducing adult people from the ANC, the other one was Lawrence Nzanga from Dube. He came and gave us a lecture about the ANC, then he started giving us Marxist literature and ANC literature and then we started reading about the struggle itself. But now what frustrated us there was no action, it was politics, politics.'

After months of political education, Zikalala and his comrades began to recruit more young people from Orlando and Diepkloof. At this point, the network began to adopt a more formal structure, with cells consisting of between five and ten people each, and soon extended its operations to other parts of Soweto and the country. At its height in 1969, Zikalala estimates there were about 300 people involved in the network. But this growth also brought them to the attention of the security police, who detained many of its leading members in May 1969 and charged them under the Terrorism Act. Although they were acquitted, the state continued to hold a number of them in detention. For example, Winnie Mandela was kept in solitary confinement for 491 days. These arrests and the consequent demise of the group effectively ended attempts to maintain an underground network in the country, but only for a few years. By the early 1970s a new generation of activists, many of whom had no prior contact with the liberation movements, began to organise clandestinely.

Kgalema Motlanthe was a central figure in one of these initiatives in Soweto. According to his biographer, in the early 1970s Kgalema and a few of his friends decided to establish a 'support group', the main aim of which was to assist those threatened with deportation to a Bantustan by the West Rand Administration Board. There was nothing overtly political about this work and the group was focused on providing humanitarian relief to the affected people. But the political landscape was changing, with more young people contemplating becoming active in resistance politics. Sometime in 1973 or 1974, Kgalema Motlanthe, Siphiwe Nyanda, Stan Nkosi and George Nene came to the conclusion that they should constitute a political cell, with the aim, first, of engaging in intense political education. Like other cells being established around Soweto at the time, they imbibed radical literature. They rented a room in a coalyard in White City, Soweto, to hold their meetings. In due course the group decided to make contact with the ANC so that they could become part of the organisation's armed wing, Umkhonto weSizwe. In view of the weakness or absence of ANC structures in the country, some of them undertook an exploratory trip to Botswana where they met the ANC, PAC as well as members of the Black Consciousness Movement. Eventually, Motlanthe travelled to Mozambique to establish direct contact with

Umkhonto weSizwe. This led the Soweto cell to become an important link between the exile movement and the nascent internal underground organisation.

Clearly, the political mood was changing in the townships. One of the important shifts that took place in the early 1970s was the commitment by a small but growing number of township youth to the struggle for freedom. They came to the conclusion that radical ideas, sacrifice and organisation would be required to achieve their goals. This marked the beginning of a decisive break with the political lull of the post-Sharpeville period. The story of Sekuthi, Ramokgopa and their comrades from Orlando reflected this political sea-change. After their experience with the principal of their school, Morris Issacson, and the authorities, the group took the critical decision to change their *modus operandi*. First, they realised that it was still too easy for 'the system' to isolate and silence critics: 'We sat down and figured out, we said guys you see this SASM thing is going to put us in trouble. Now already we've seen that when we trying to use this and it filtered easily and it ended up … We talk about this now exposed, we will be easily victimised, silenced, things like that.'

Based on their assessment of the situation, the group came to the conclusion that they should 'try to operate, go underground. We decided now what we are going to do, we are going to operate as a close unit and call those unit cells.' Sekuthi explains what they did next: 'Then we formed a Soweto Seven. It was myself, Sydney Ramokgopa, Oupa Motlana, Raymond Pilane, Amos Masondo, Joe the elderly guy, [and] Roy Masinga. We assigned duties to each other. And then first it was we are going to split but not necessarily split, but one has to go out and organise four people and form a cell, and then other one would be introduced. So now that man that this one is a police a watchdog, he wants to see that you really organised, you have organised four people so he must go and see, that this cell has been organised. All of us we had to go out and then one has to introduce this other cell. So we spread like that, kind of thing that … so we had a mother body and we would sit down and we would now, all that we would make up, we would come up with policies, decide what to do, what not to do if things like that. And we said then we need to organise literature to politicise ourselves and then this literature more especially banned literature … started to … go to the other cells.'

It is unclear how much success the 'Soweto Seven' had in spreading their underground network. One of the first things they did was to organise a trip to Botswana with the aim of getting a sense of the state of the exile political movements and obtain more banned literature. Here they met Clarence Hamilton, who was a member of a semi-clandestine network based in the neighbouring Soweto suburb of Noordgesig. After their return to Orlando, the group again came to the attention of the security police, which led to the arrest and subsequent torture of Amos

Masondo. At this point, several members, including Sekuthi and Ramokgopa, decided to go into exile to avoid imprisonment. Their decision to skip the country happened to coincide with reports of protests by students directed primarily against the state's decision to impose Afrikaans as a medium of instruction in all African schools.

3

'To hell with Afrikaans'

The apartheid government's insistence on introducing Afrikaans as a medium of instruction in African schools, a product of ideological hubris, was a political miscalculation of historic proportions. When the decision was taken in the early 1970s, the ruling National Party was arguably at the pinnacle of its power and apartheid appeared to be unassailable. In the late 1960s, the government had come under pressure to expand the provision of secondary schooling to Africans to meet industry's need for a more skilled labour force. While conceding the necessity of this shift in policy, the government was determined to do so within the parameters of Bantu Education, a cornerstone of the apartheid system. This education system sought to entrench the secondary status of Africans by producing young African men and women who would be qualified for employment only in the lower levels of the economy. It aimed to inhibit the aspirations of young black people and to prepare them to serve the needs of the white population. To meet these objectives, apartheid ideologues argued, Africans had to be taught in the

languages of whites: English and Afrikaans.

This was a long-standing policy, though the Department of Bantu Education generally granted African schools exemption from having to use Afrikaans as a medium of instruction. But driven by the desire to impose its ideological dominance, the government in the early 1970s moved decisively to entrench the use of Afrikaans. In response to criticisms, the Secretary for Bantu Education set out the logic of the state's new policy directive: 'In urban areas the education of a Black child is being paid for by the White population, that is English- and Afrikaans-speaking groups. Therefore the Secretary for Bantu Education has a responsibility towards the English- and Afrikaans-speaking people. Consequently, the only way of satisfying both groups, the medium of instruction in all schools shall be on a 50-50 basis.' Not surprisingly, in the eyes of young black people Afrikaans came to symbolise apartheid oppression.

The state's determination to pursue its ideological objectives at the expense of African children's education acted as the catalyst for mounting discontent in Soweto and other townships. As the previous chapter explains, the early 1970s witnessed a rebirth of resistance politics. On the eve of the uprising the various networks, groups and organisations spawned in the preceding few years remained relatively weak and fragmented. But opposition to Afrikaans galvanised these forces. Despite objections, first from parents and then more vociferously from students, the government doggedly adhered to its policy. And when students in Soweto began to protest, the authorities either dismissed their complaints or tried to suppress them. Even when teachers and students pointed to the deleterious impact the policy would have on the quality of education, politicians from the ruling party simply reiterated their ideological stance.

Parents raised their objections eighteen months before the uprising, largely limiting them to appeals and the submission of memoranda to the authorities. Student mobilisation against the introduction of Afrikaans commenced at the start of the academic year in 1976. These nascent struggles were organised by individual schools and were mostly short-lived. Moreover, as Sifiso Ndlovu has argued, the students who were in the forefront of the campaign were those directly affected by the new medium of instruction, namely, those in Forms One and Two in the junior secondary schools. Local school committees led these campaigns and over time some of them coalesced into inter-school co-ordinating structures, the most important being the Action Committee, launched three days before the uprising. For the most part, the young leaders of the campaign against Afrikaans in the first half of 1976 were disconnected from existing movements and political groups like the BCM or SASM.

It is absolutely important to recognise that the struggle against Afrikaans did not happen suddenly on 16 June 1976. In fact, that fateful day can be viewed as the culmination of months of appeals, protests and sporadic confrontations with the police. Nonetheless, the unprecedented involvement of thousands of students on the march and the subsequent riot on 16 June caught most South Africans (and indeed the world) by surprise. Consequently, the uprising has been described as a spontaneous outburst of anger by black students. It is a view to which both the state and white society in general readily subscribed at the time. Black protests were deemed irrational, disorderly and destructive. Moreover, in the white view, young township students were incapable of formulating political demands or organising protests, and responsibility was therefore pinned on outside 'agitators' who were allegedly behind the rebellion. As we shall see, white people's prejudices blinded them to the crisis unfolding in Soweto's schools throughout 1976.

The focus of this chapter is on the initial two phases of opposition to the implementation of Afrikaans as a vehicle of instruction, namely, from late 1974 to the end of 1975 and the first half of 1976. In this way, it is possible to gain better insight into the changing character of the protests, including their shifting generational dimensions. As the limitation of appeals to the Department of Bantu Education became obvious, the tone of objections, including from some adults, grew more strident. Perhaps most crucially, the intensification of the struggle from early 1976 was led by young black students, the majority of whom had no previous political experience. Throughout this period, the white authorities maintained their ideological intransigence and were impervious to appeals even from moderate voices in the township. Their standard responses to objections raised by parents and students were to dismiss them and, when further opposition was raised, to silence the voices of dissent through intimidation.

The arrogance of the state in dealing with the legitimate concerns of students and parents is sometimes ignored as a critical cause of the radicalisation of students. The existence of large numbers of urbanised black youth with access, for the first time, to high school education (albeit one with severe problems) engendered a strong desire to use education as one means to overcome the limitations imposed on them by apartheid. Dikeledi Motswene, who attended Ithute Junior Secondary School in 1976, had high hopes. 'I wanted to be something. I wanted to be a scientist. You know why I wanted to be a scientist? I wanted to mix things, but because my parents were not having enough money, I didn't go too far. I dropped.' Solly Mphse wanted to use his education to improve his family's condition: 'You know my main aim was just to pass, progress, to become something in order to help my mom, because she was suffering and all that. We became confused, because of Afrikaans.' Sibongile Mkhabela has described Naledi High School as the 'jewel of the wild west' where the principal at the time, Mr Rudolph Mthimkhulu, 'instilled ... a sense of purpose, ambition, drive, self-love, and a vision of the possible'. Teachers set 'high standards for academic performance' and students were 'highly competitive'. Her commerce class of 1976 'wanted to prove that we were as capable, if not more capable, than the "A"-class students who were enrolled for maths and physics'. Students understood that the introduction of Afrikaans would further undermine township schooling. Overall, there was a growing sense that the apartheid state wanted to destroy the already limited educational opportunities for black youth.

Parents voice their objections
Black parents have been roundly criticised for their apparent compliance and silence in the aftermath of the

Sharpeville massacre. They have even been accused of acquiescing in apartheid and being cowed into submission by state repression. Their apparent silence over the issue of Afrikaans has also been contrasted with the militancy of the students' rebellion. However, it would be wrong to assume that parents or teachers did not object to the state's policy on Afrikaans. They were among the first to voice opposition, but they did so mainly within existing official structures. *The World* captured the prevailing mood among African parents on this issue: 'Whether the South African government likes it or not, many urban African parents are bitterly opposed to their children being forced to learn in Afrikaans. We can well appreciate that this may be a sore point with a Government dedicated to propagating Afrikaans. But the objection of these parents is well founded.'

When the authorities in 1974 issued a circular announcing the compulsory implementation of Afrikaans as a medium of instruction, township-based school boards immediately raised objections. Until then school boards had routinely applied for exemption from the state's language policy, which was invariably granted. However, in December 1974 the Orlando-Diepkloof Zulu School Board's application for exemption was rejected without reason. This was a clear signal of the state's unilateral decision to terminate the status quo, and propelled the usually compliant members of school boards into action. A few days before Christmas nearly a hundred delegates representing school boards from the entire PWV region met in the Pretoria township of Atteridgeville to consider the government's intransigent application of its language policy. There was reportedly general disappointment about the authorities' refusal to grant exemption, which led to the expression of disapproval from many of the delegates. Opposition from the school boards was highly unusual. The mounting frustration was reflected in a speech by Mr M. Peta, a prominent member of the Atteridgeville School Board. Using language that would have been unfamiliar to his audience, he declared: 'We have to be militant to be understood. We have been docile for too long. If the Department says no to our demands, our children must stay away from schools next year.' These views reflected the growing indignation among parents. In the end, however, Peta's rather radical recommendation did not gain majority support. Instead, the various boards decided to submit a memorandum of demands to the Department of Bantu Education. But their pleas fell on deaf ears. In response to this official rebuff, a smaller group of school boards convened a meeting in Sharpeville, where a more strident tone was evident among delegates. A proposed meeting in neighbouring Sebokeng was banned by the circuit inspector, indicating a hardening in the attitude of the Department of Bantu Education in dealing with any form of opposition. In sum, the concerted efforts by school boards at the end of 1974 to dissuade the authorities from pursuing their plans proved mostly ineffective and futile.

The seriousness with which boards approached this problem was reflected in the decision by the Orlando-Diepkloof Zulu Board, led by Mr J. Mahlangu, to draft a document which carefully spelt out the serious pedagogical problems inherent in the Afrikaans language policy. It seemed obvious to the school boards that forcing African children to learn subjects in Afrikaans would hamper their education. But the government again refused to consider their concerns. Mr Mahlangu now took the highly unusual step of defying the authorities and invoked what he believed was the board's authority to determine certain educational policies for the schools under its jurisdiction. He instructed teachers to use only English as a medium at the beginning of the academic year in 1975. The Department of Bantu Education not only saw this as a provocation but also insisted that Mr Mahlangu had overstepped the bounds of his authority. It summarily dismissed him, thereby sending a clear signal that it would not tolerate dissent.

Teachers' organisations also entered the fray. In early January 1975 the African Teachers' Association of South Africa (ATASA) sent a memorandum to the Department of Bantu Education asking it to reconsider its decision and take into account the views of African people. But the department was adamant it would continue with its policy. Punt Janson, the Deputy Minister, was characteristically unapologetic about the government's approach on this matter: 'No, I have not consulted the African people on the language issue and I'm not going to ... I have consulted the Constitution of the Republic of South Africa ... The leaders of the various homelands can in due course decide what they want to do in their own homelands where they are the masters. However, as far as the white areas are concerned this is a decision that has been taken and I am going to stand by it.'

Although the department's assertion of white authority seemed to force ATASA to retreat, simmering anger within black society was becoming more evident. The extent of the prevailing mood was reflected in an editorial in *The World* on 6 January 1975: 'Why should we in the urban areas have Afrikaans – a language spoken nowhere else in the world and which is still in a raw state of development, in any case – pushed down our throats? The implications of this new directive are too serious to leave now. We urge parents to join forces with teachers all over the country and fight the directive. The Government must be left in no doubt at all about how seriously we view their highhanded action ... The situation can only deteriorate further unless the new regulations are scrapped.'

Although opposition from school boards dissipated in 1975, the state's decision to proceed with its plan in 1976 triggered a new round of disputes, the most important occurring between the Department of Education and the Tswana School Board in Meadowlands. In January

1976 the school board formally objected to the Afrikaans policy but was rudely dismissed by the circuit inspector, who told its members that they had no right to comment on matters related to African education in 'white South Africa'. And, echoing the official position, he informed them that the government, and whites in general, would decide what to do with schooling for Africans. The only concession the authorities seemed prepared to consider was to allow schools to apply for an exemption, but insisted that any successful application would be valid only for a year, after which Afrikaans would be automatically implemented.

At this point the Tswana School Board concluded that appeals to the authorities would serve no purpose and, following the example of their colleagues in the Orlando-Diepkloof Zulu Board the previous year, resolved that English would be the main medium of instruction. Predictably, the Department of Education responded swiftly to quash this challenge to its authority and dismissed the chairman, Mr Peele. His replacement, Mr Letlape, refused to accede to the demands of the department and was also summarily dismissed. The seven remaining board members resigned in solidarity with their colleagues and, crucially, students at the school boycotted classes to demand the reinstatement of the board members. This stand-off reflected the deep frustration prevalent in the school boards of Soweto. But it also exposed their inherent weakness: ultimately they did not possess any real authority to make decisions in the interest of the schools nominally under their jurisdiction. That power was firmly in the hands of the Department of Bantu Education. By treating the boards with such utter disdain, the government in fact confirmed the widely held view that the boards were toothless bodies.

By ignoring the appeals from two constituencies directly involved in township education – parents and teachers – the state confirmed its willingness to sacrifice black education on the altar of ideological arrogance. In so doing, it alienated groups of adults who were traditionally moderate in their political views. Parents and teachers had tried for more than a year to stop a policy that was obviously disastrous, but had failed. It was now left to the students to challenge the authorities.

The struggle gains momentum

In a rare moment of objectivity, the Cillie Commission of Inquiry admitted in its final report that 'There is no doubt about it that there was dissatisfaction in Soweto about the question of Afrikaans as a medium of instruction'. Of course the authorities, especially in the Department of Bantu Education, were well aware of the opposition to Afrikaans, but, at best, remained unwilling to acknowledge the deep anger towards its policies and, at worst, simply did not care. Having weathered the moderate and intermittent protests from the school boards, the authorities began systematically to implement the new language policy from the beginning of 1976. Students in Forms One and Two in Soweto's secondary schools were among the first to be confronted with Afrikaans as a medium of instruction when they entered their classrooms at the start of the academic year. Education suffered immediately because teachers were expected to teach in a language most of them could not even speak. Mrs Sithole, who had more than twenty years of teaching experience in Soweto, explained that her colleagues were baffled by the language: 'To be honest, Afrikaans was also a problem even to us teachers. Just imagine teaching mathematics in Afrikaans. That was totally insane. We couldn't do it. We would laugh about it and crack jokes like, "come let us count: *een, twee, drie* ... [laughs]. What do you call 'plus' in Afrikaans?"'

This basic pedagogical problem was hardly a surprise. In 1973 the Department of Bantu Education had experimented by introducing Afrikaans for a limited number of subjects in selected schools. One of the affected schools was in Tembisa. Figo Madlala, who was at Tembisa High in 1973, remembers how difficult it was for his teacher to explain the most basic terms in agricultural studies (*landbou*) in Form One. Three years later none of the underlying problems associated with the introduction of Afrikaans were resolved. To make matters worse, subjects such as mathematics, history and geography would now be taught in Afrikaans. Paul Ndaba, who attended Phefeni Junior Secondary, expressed a universally held frustration about the situation confronting students: 'Firstly the language itself was a problem, you would get a word in mathematics being said in Afrikaans, like "algebra", and this word in Afrikaans is a word I cannot even understand. You come to biology, geography ... all those words. The words for the instruments that we have to use [in the lab] were just not on. Those words were just difficult. Secondly, the teachers themselves were not well equipped to teach these subjects in Afrikaans. They were just able to teach Afrikaans as language ... The marks that we got when we did all these three subjects in Afrikaans were extremely bad. We saw that we're not getting anywhere.'

Tebogo Tsenase remembers 'that [what] really pissed everybody' was being informed that most subjects would be taught in Afrikaans by the time they reached matric. With students directly experiencing the adverse effects of instruction through Afrikaans, the opposition to the language policy gained new momentum. One of the first reported incidents of protest took place at Thomas Mofolo Secondary School on 24 February, when students confronted the principal about the introduction of Afrikaans. Students threatened to escalate their protests if they did not receive a satisfactory answer to their concerns, but the police were called in to intervene. Although the protest was immediately quelled, tensions continued to simmer at the school.

Members of the BPC and SASO decided at a meeting

in Orlando East to speak to the principal at Mofolo about holding a public meeting to address the problem, but nothing seems to have come of this initiative. No doubt aware of the problems being caused by the introduction of Afrikaans, parents re-entered the fray. On 13 March, parents at Diepkloof Junior Secondary formally raised their objections to the system and decided to apply for exemption. The following day, parents at Donaldson Higher Primary also unanimously rejected the plan. Responding to the growing frustration experienced by teachers, the African Teachers' Association of South Africa met the Secretary for Bantu Education to hand over a memorandum. But, as before, this overture to settle the brewing crisis was dismissed by the authorities.

Between March and mid-May there were further reports of student protests and formal objections raised by parents and teachers. For the most part these actions were localised and aimed at resolving the language crisis at particular schools. Political organisations were mostly absent or, at best, only intermittently involved in the emerging campaign. As yet there seemed to be no plan to unite the disparate protests into a single, township-wide campaign – a reflection of the fragmented nature of protest politics in Soweto at the time. Police intervened quickly and often violently to quell protests, which made it even more difficult to mobilise a broader struggle. Furthermore, some principals and teachers colluded with the authorities to identify and silence protesting students.

With mid-year examinations on the horizon, it appeared the authorities had largely succeeded in suppressing the outbreak of local protests. But it was precisely the prospect of poor academic performance in the examinations that galvanised students into stepping up the struggle. At the centre of this critical shift in the struggle by Soweto students was Phefeni Junior Secondary School.

Phefeni Junior Secondary leads the way

Sifiso Ndlovu has written insightfully about the uprising of 1976 and especially the crucial role played by his alma mater, Phefeni Junior Secondary School, in the month before the rebellion broke out. He was a 14-year-old in Form Two in 1976 and recalled that students from Forms One and Two had been discussing their response to Afrikaans from as early as March: 'we dedicated the afternoon lesson in our class, from 2 o'clock to about 4 o'clock, to discussions about the directive that Afrikaans should be the medium of instruction in our schools … It is worth noting that this only affected Form One and Form Two. The senior students – that is, Form Three in our school and at high schools throughout Soweto – were excluded. These afternoon sessions were out of bounds for our prefects (except for one Seth Mazibuko), for teachers and other authorities including the principal, Mr Mpulo.'

Affected students first employed a 'go slow' tactic to bring their dissatisfaction to the school's attention. After receiving 'disheartening feedback and low marks from the various subjects that used Afrikaans', the students decided to take a firm stand. For Ndlovu and his peers this was a critically important matter. They were performing well at school and had aspirations not only to achieve good matric results but possibly to study further. Many of them had enrolled for science-related subjects, in the belief that this would improve their chances in the world of work and of enrolling for tertiary education. But these were precisely the subjects that were now taught in Afrikaans. Students interpreted the new medium of instruction as a direct assault by the government on the prospects for advancement by young black people.

Teachers at the school also signed a petition to voice their opposition, while students made efforts to negotiate with the school authorities. Initially, students were aggrieved by the refusal of the Department of Bantu Education to meet them. When they were eventually granted an audience, it was with low-ranking officials and staff at the school, who had no power to reverse the policy. Students concluded quite soon that it was futile to negotiate with the education authorities. There also appears to have been very little, if any, involvement by parents or the local school boards in the matter.

The students' sense of isolation was compounded in the early stages of their campaign by a perceived lack of support from senior students. In fact, Ndlovu insists that 'Students from the various high schools in Soweto were not at first interested in our plight and struggle, as they were using English as a medium of instruction. They carried on with their studies as if nothing was happening during the formative, crucial days leading to the uprising.' Even the senior students at Phefeni, the Form Threes, seemed uninterested in their plight. From the perspectives of the students who were at the coalface of the campaign against Afrikaans, those who would later assume the mantle of leadership of the uprising were quite removed from the initial struggles. 'I do not remember', Ndlovu has written, 'any liberation movement, such as the Black Consciousness Movement or the South African Students Movement (SASM), contributing to our daily meetings and discussions.'

During these early days of the struggle, Seth Mazibuko, a senior student at Phefeni Secondary School, was the only recognised student leader directly involved in the unfolding campaign. He was connected to political activists from other schools and, as the struggle intensified and spread to other junior secondary schools, he played a pivotal co-ordinating role. He also served as the vital link between participants in these struggles and established student activists. It was to him the students at Phefeni turned with a letter that set out their concerns. Their request for a meeting with the circuit inspector, Mr De Beer, to hand over their letter was dismissed. At this point Phefeni students decided to embark on a different course of action.

Faced by intransigent authorities and a lack of

support from their fellows, the students at Phefeni decided to embark on a class boycott from 16 May. The adoption of this tactic was arguably the high point of the first phase in the students' struggle against Afrikaans and inaugurated a process of contestation that would culminate in the rebellion exactly a month later. Events now unfolded at a quicker pace than in the preceding four months. Boycotting students drafted a five-point memorandum to the principal, Mr Charles Mpulo, and sent a letter of grievance to the Bantu Education regional director. Tensions escalated at the school when the vice-principal, Mr F. Nhlapo, was found with a tape-recorder. He was immediately accused of being a police informer and threatened with violence, but was rescued by the intervention of the principal. Relations between the students and the school's leadership deteriorated even further when the chairman of the school board, Mr Ngwenya, failed to address the students as promised, and as a result students vented their anger by stoning the principal's office.

Importantly, the struggle at Phefeni quickly spread to other schools. On 19 May, schools in the surrounding area, such as Belle, Thulasizwe, Emthonjeni and Khulangolwazi, launched a solidarity boycott, involving approximately 1600 students. As part of the protest, about 300 students from Thulasizwe marched through the area singing, 'Thulasizwe is tired of Afrikaans, this language must go from this school.' At this time, Ndlovu suggests, a co-ordinating body was established, based primarily on the junior secondary schools, which attempted to unite these separate struggles. It appears that Seth Mazibuko was a central figure in these efforts. There is also some indication that schools from other parts of Soweto became involved in local protests. On 24 May, 300 pupils from Pimville Higher Primary joined the boycott and stuck a placard, with the iconic slogan 'To hell with Afrikaans', on the school gate. Four days after the start of the boycott the principal agreed to a meeting with the students, but it ended in deadlock, as he was unable or unwilling to make a commitment to the withdrawal of Afrikaans.

As the crisis at Phefeni School deepened, other sectors of black society intervened to caution the government on the political consequences if it failed to address the students' concerns. The usually compliant Urban Bantu Council of Soweto went so far as to warn the authorities of the dangers of a repeat of the Sharpeville crisis. Councillor Leonard Mosala admitted that the children 'won't take anything we say because they think we have neglected them. We have failed to help them in their struggle for change in schools. They are now angry and prepared to fight and we are afraid the situation may become chaotic at any time.' An even more strident critique was issued by Mr W.B. Ngakane of the South African Council of Churches, who lambasted the 'stupidity of Bantu Education officials' in their handling of the crisis at Phefeni. He warned the 'Afrikaner' that they had 'created an attitude of hate on the part of the Black man'. 'By forcing Black children to learn maths and science in Afrikaans,' Ngakane was quoted as saying in *The World*, 'the authorities are giving Black pupils their first lesson in solidarity.'

Despite the mounting outcry from various quarters, the authorities remained unperturbed by the events unfolding in Soweto. No one represented the Nero-like attitude more than Andries Treurnicht, the Deputy Minister of Education and arch-conservative in the ruling party. In a letter responding to concerns raised by the South African Institute of Race Relations (SAIRR), Treurnicht wrote, 'The problem in connection with the strike by pupils in Soweto are still being dealt with at a lower level, and apparently negotiations have not yet ended in deadlock … We shall ascertain what the root causes are, but at the moment it is said that the children are striking because teachers (according to the children?) are not competent to teach subjects in Afrikaans. Perhaps it is not quite so simple.'

The state very likely hoped the school boycott would not last, especially with the examinations looming. In fact, during the first week of June it appeared that the strike at some schools was losing momentum: pupils at Emthonjeni, Belle, Thulasizwe and Pimville began to return to class. The authorities appeared to have made a minor concession to the students at Emthonjeni and Belle, giving them the assurance that mathematics and social studies would not be immediately taught in

Afrikaans. As a result the militancy previously witnessed at these schools quickly dissipated. But the state's main response to the protests was to break the resistance through intimidation and direct police action. The respected principal of Orlando High, Mr T.W. Kambule, complained that the circuit inspector, Mr De Beer, was intimidating teachers and principals at the schools where boycotts were taking place. But this did not deter students. On the contrary, they now fought back when the police invaded their schools. Incidents at Pimville Higher Primary and Naledi, where students confronted the police, were harbingers of the conflict that would ensue in months to come.

Despite the state's efforts to break the boycott, the students at Phefeni Junior Secondary stood firm. With the examinations around the corner, the boycotting students took the critical decision not to write. In their view, the academic year had already been forfeited because of the state's policies and its refusal to accede to the demand to drop Afrikaans. They had nothing more to lose that year. Boycotting students then turned their attention to mobilising support from senior students at the school. Paul Ndaba explains what followed: 'What happened was that the Form Threes were fully aware of the situation … There was no other way but for them to join us and guide us or help us [as seniors] to get the problem sorted out. But the way things were going, they would be with us at a particular time and be on the other side at another particular time. We expected them to down their pens. We wanted full sympathy from them, not half-baked type of thing. They carried on with their studies [and began to write their exams during the first week of June] whilst nothing was being resolved, so we decided to go into the exams room and tore up the exam papers, and forced them out the classroom. That is exactly when things started to get sour now – they then officially joined us because they had no option.'

For the first time in the campaign against Afrikaans, students demonstrated a determination to sacrifice their own schooling for the bigger cause. Moreover, they were prepared to use any means necessary to persuade their colleagues to take a stand with them. Mr Kambule, the Orlando High principal, captured the emerging mood in Soweto in early June 1976: 'If teachers in the junior high schools accept or are forced to use Afrikaans then the Government will have a good case in forcing Afrikaans as the medium of instruction in high schools. School children are doing exactly what the parents and everybody feels about Afrikaans – only they had the courage to stand up against it.'

SASM steps in

SASM's leaders in Soweto mainly comprised senior students from the high schools who were not directly affected by the Afrikaans policy. Consequently they – and, by extension, SASM – were not initially involved in the struggles led by the junior students. Although SASM as an organisation continued to struggle to survive, there is evidence that in early 1976 it was making efforts to launch branches in high schools. By mid-year the appeals by junior students for seniors to join their struggle compelled the latter to take a stand. Moreover, the struggle against Afrikaans had asserted itself as a critical issue in Soweto as a whole and was being addressed by a growing number of organisations, including the Black Consciousness Movement. In the circumstances, SASM inevitably entered the fray.

Sibongile Mkhabela's political development in 1976 reflected broader processes among young people in Soweto, as well as the increasing involvement of SASM in the evolving crisis. She quickly rose through the ranks of SASM to become its national general secretary, in an indication of the important role played at the time by young women in student politics and later also in the uprising. A turning point in her development as a political activist was a commemoration service on the anniversary of the Sharpeville massacre, organised by SASO and BPC. This event had 'an immense psychological impact' on her. It was then that she decided to commit herself to the cause of liberation. Like many young people at the time, Mkhabela aligned herself with the 'militant Black Consciousness philosophy'.

Her recollection of the first part of 1976 was that it was a 'normal year'. 'The school programme continued, we played sports, we won debates against our rivals, we laughed and teased, we did our homework ...' While Mkhabela certainly knew about the police intervention at the junior schools, the struggle against Afrikaans did not directly affect students at Naledi High.

However, the school was eventually thrust into the students' struggle on 8 June 1976, a few weeks after the junior schools embarked on boycotts. On that day the police entered the school and attempted to arrest Enos Ngutshana, the SASM secretary at the school. Students reacted to the provocation by burning the police car and forced the policemen to barricade themselves inside the principal's office. In the ensuing chaos Ngutshana managed to escape. A large contingent of police reinforcements arrived to rescue their colleagues. In the process students and police confronted each other, the one group armed with stones, the other with guns and teargas. Senior students were increasingly being drawn into the struggle, and SASM correspondingly assumed a more active role.

Ten days before the incident at Naledi High, SASM had in fact already recognised that Afrikaans represented an important issue. At its annual General Students' Council meeting held in Roodepoort on 28–30 May, the organisation discussed the implications of the state's language policy. The gathering criticised Bantu Education as a whole and Afrikaans in particular. A resolution passed at the conference sent a strong and unambiguous message of support to the junior students:

> The recent strike by schools against the use of Afrikaans as a medium of instruction is a sign of demonstration against schools systematised to producing 'good industrial boys' for the powers that be ... We therefore resolve to totally reject the use of Afrikaans as a medium of instruction, to fully support the students who took the stand in the rejection of this dialect [and] also to condemn the racially separated education system.
>
> Noted,
>
> 1. The strikes that been going on in Soweto against Afrikaans being used as the medium of instruction.
> 2. Its national implications to Black people in this country.
>
> Resolved,
>
> 1. To fully pledge on solidarity with the schools on strike against Afrikaans being used as a medium of instruction.
> 2. To actively sympathise with those schools on strike.

Murphy Morobe, who joined SASM in 1974 and was one of its key figures in 1976, has explained that the movement viewed Afrikaans as an important issue around which to mobilise students in the struggle against Bantu Education as a whole. SASM thus sent a strong signal of its intention to become more directly involved in the campaign against Afrikaans. The Roodepoort conference did not formulate a concrete plan of action. But the escalation of struggles, especially at Phefeni School, prompted the SASM leadership to intervene. SASM contacted the co-ordinating committee of the junior secondary schools, and a decision was taken to convene a meeting of student representatives from all over Soweto on Sunday, 13 June at the Donaldson Community Centre in Orlando East. This was an historic meeting at which student activists committed themselves to support those involved in boycott by organising solidarity action by the rest of the township's students.

Mkhabela recalls the mood and some of the issues discussed at the meeting: 'Tempers flared high at the meeting, for we all felt it was time we took action ... Pupils shared stories about cruel police activities in their school. In some schools there was clear collaboration between members of staff and the police, but most school administrators had remained supportive of their pupils ... Students did not hate school; this I felt in my bones and soul. Rather, school was being taken away from Black pupils.' Seth Mazibuko recalled a year later that 'The main speaker was a man called Aubrey who explained to us what the aims and objects of SASM were. He also discussed the use of Afrikaans as a means of tuition or language and called upon the prefects of our schools to come forward and to explain what the position was there.

I stood up and told the congregation that the Phefeni School refused to use Afrikaans and they had boycotted classes during May 1976.'

This seems to have been a turning point in the meeting, as students now turned their attention to consider concrete solidarity action. According to Mazibuko, 'Aubrey then enquired how could other schools support us in our stand as they were writing exams and Phefeni was not.' At that point another charismatic student leader addressed the meeting: 'Don [Tsietsi] Mashinini suggested that a mass demonstration should be held on 16.6.76 by all black schools.' The proposal was endorsed by the meeting and immediately an Action Committee, comprising members of the SASM leadership and the junior secondary schools' co-ordinating committee, was established. Among its members were Tsietsi Mashinini, Murphy Morobe, Seth Mazibuko, David Kutumela and Isaiah Molefe. The Action Committee was given responsibility to plan the demonstration and at the end of the meeting it convened briefly to begin preparations for the demonstration three days later. It met again the following day, when more detailed plans and demands were formulated. The scene was now set for the historic march on 16 June.

4

16 June 1976
From protest to riot

The students' march on 16 June and the state's violent response completely transformed not only the protest against Afrikaans in Soweto but the whole nature of politics in South Africa. Events on that day may be divided into two distinct phases, separated by a volley of police bullets that reverberated across the world. Between 7 and 8 am students began to gather at their schools, from where they embarked on a series of peaceful protest marches through the streets of Soweto. At some time between 10 and 11 am the police's deadly intervention provoked widespread anger among the students, triggering a riot that engulfed most sections of the township and lasted until late in the evening. Informed by police reports, the official narrative of these events accused students of instigating the violence and sought to blame outside 'agitators' – the exiled ANC and PAC, as well as the BPC – for being behind the demonstration. The Cillie Commission of Inquiry later reiterated the hackneyed script of the apartheid government and attempted to absolve the state not only of creating the conditions that caused the protest but of the deadly violence itself.

Oral testimonies collected from a wide range of participants, principally from the main actors, the students, have punched holes in this official narrative. There now exists a rich oral history archive as well as a series of publications based on it that has produced new insights into the events as they unfolded on 16 June. What has emerged from these testimonies is the pivotal role played by the Action Committee in planning the peaceful demonstration against the use of Afrikaans. Established only three days before the protest, it had very little time to mobilise properly, but it succeeded in tapping into the groundswell of discontent among students to garner unprecedented support for the day of action. Nevertheless, the Action Committee's reach into the schools was understandably limited, which meant that many students, especially in the lower grades, were not aware of the plan of action. On the day, however, thousands joined the various marches to express their objection to the state's language policy and more broadly to Bantu Education. It turned out to be the largest demonstration in Soweto since the mass campaigns that preceded the Sharpeville massacre in 1960.

Preparing for the protest
Members of the Action Committee spent Monday and Tuesday speaking to groups of students and trusted

activists at several schools to inform them of the plans for the march on Wednesday, 16 June. Their main message was clear: students had to mobilise *en masse* to send an unambiguous statement to the authorities about their rejection of Afrikaans as a medium of instruction. In addition to spreading the word about the demonstration, students were asked to produce placards denouncing Afrikaans. Finally, and importantly, students were told not to inform their parents about the march. According to Sibongile Mkhabela, attendees at the meeting on the 13th made 'a pact that parents should not be involved. They should not even be told about what was going to happen on the 16th. Given the multitudes of students who were there, it was actually surprising to find that we all went home and kept quiet.' The Action Committee was primarily concerned to keep their plans secret from the authorities, anticipating that they would attempt to intimidate students. But student leaders were also anxious that parents, worried about the safety of their children and generally reticent about protests, would try to prevent them from proceeding with the march.

As the sun rose on the winter morning of 16 June there was little indication of the historic events that would explode on the streets of Soweto later that day. Most parents had little or no idea of the students' planned march. A normal day of work lay ahead, or so they thought. Elliott Ndlovu, father of Hastings Ndlovu, who was one of the first victims of police action on 16

June, explained that he 'woke up as usual. I did not know anything, these kids were too secretive.' Dan Moyane remembers student leaders appealing to them 'not to make our parents aware'. On the morning of the 16th, he meticulously followed the household rituals so as not to raise his parents' suspicions. Moyane knew the charade was successful when his mother told him before she left: 'Hey, child, here's money for bread. When you come back, eat!' But as soon as his parents left for work, 'I took my placard … we weren't taking books.' Similar routines were repeated in homes across the township as uninformed parents made ready for work and their children prepared to make history.

Although the Action Committee was remarkably successful in mobilising students, it simply did not have enough time to visit all the schools in Soweto. Inevitably, therefore, many students were unaware of the march. This was especially the case for those in the lower standards. Dikeledi Motswene, who attended Ithute Junior Secondary School, only learnt about the event when a close schoolmate told her to leave her school bag at home because they were going on a march. She was surprised and 'just confused, really I was confused' about whether to join the demonstration. But Motswene was also curious and decided to join her friend. Erick Ngobeni, who attended Ngungunyane Junior Secondary School, was even more ignorant of the planned march. 'I woke up, as usual, like all other days. I ate soft porridge because it was our usual breakfast … After that I took my books. I usually left home at half past seven, because our school was a little far away. I went to collect my friend who stayed nearby. He was called Ronald Rikhotso. Then we went to school just like the other days.' Some parents did find out about the march from their children and kept them at home.

It is impossible to determine the success of the Action Committee's attempts to reach all students. Considering the size of Soweto and the sheer number of schools in the township, it was to be expected that not everyone could be reached in the two days available for organisation. High schools where SASM had a presence and the junior secondary schools that had been involved in the struggles against Afrikaans were quite easily organised. Groupings of activists and rudimentary organisations existed in these schools, and could be relatively quickly harnessed to the cause. Beyond this core cluster, mobilisation was uneven. Some parts of Soweto, including Orlando East, were not reached at all by the Action Committee and primary schools were deliberately excluded from the initial mobilisation.

On the eve of the march there was a growing mood of excitement and expectation among those in the know. Students sensed they were on the verge of making history. Teboho Mohape was informed about the planned demonstration prior to 16 June and expected a 'very peaceful march'. In the day or two before, he and his friends 'were talking about what a surprise it was going to be to our parents and teachers. They would just see us walking out of class and would try to stop us and then we would tell them "Wait, this is our day".'

On the morning of the 16th, leaders of the Action Committee were involved in frenetic activity to ensure there would be maximum participation. A number of them went from school to school to address student assemblies. Murphy Morobe spoke to students at Rhulane Senior Primary. Vusi Zwane, a student at the school, heard the senior student activist explain the reasons behind the march. Morobe then called on them to join and appealed to them to be disciplined. 'We must be quiet' is how Zwane remembers Morobe's request. Students from this school were told to march to Elkah Stadium, where they would join other schools to listen to a speech by Tsietsi Mashinini. According to Erick Ngobeni and George Baloyi, who attended Ngungunyane Junior Secondary School, activists arrived at the school and went directly to the principal. At the same time a group of students congregated in the school yard chanting support for the demonstration. The rest of the school awaited the outcome of the deliberations with the principal. Soon after the activists left the principal's office, Ngobeni saw students streaming out of their classes to join the group singing in the yard. At that point he too decided to join the protesters as they marched out of the school.

Such scenes were repeated across Soweto. Student

leaders at Senaoane Secondary School timed their announcement of the demonstration to perfection. They waited for all the students to assemble for morning prayers and then, before the principal could address the student body, the activists 'took up the rostrum [and] explained the route that we were going to take'. The audacity of their action and the direct challenge it presented to the school authority sent waves of excitement through the student ranks. A similar plan was hatched at Naledi High School, where SASM was also influential. As they gathered for the morning assembly, students raised placards bearing slogans such as 'Afrikaans stinks'. A senior SASM member, Tebello Motapanyane, and other activists took charge and led the students to the school gates, chanting 'Power! Away with Afrikaans' and 'Free Azania, Power!' Likewise, members of the Action Committee at Morris Isaacson used the morning assembly to launch their march. As soon as they gathered in the school grounds, students started singing 'Nkosi Sikelel' iAfrika', and then marched out of the school.

Most students joined the marches voluntarily, even if they only found out about the demonstration on the morning of the 16th. But not everyone supported the protest. Mrs Mafafane, a teacher at Khotso Lower Primary, had no objection to teaching Afrikaans and opposed the student boycotts. On the morning of 16 June she was teaching Afrikaans when a student alerted her to marchers entering the school grounds. She recalls what happened next: 'There were lots of people coming from that side, they didn't care whether you were busy teaching, they knock and say "OUT! You are teaching Afrikaans?" I said, "What does Afrikaans do?" And they said, "Mam, OUT! Stop this, we don't want it, release these children now!" Then we all went out with my students, we sat outside.'

There were also reports of students being forced out of classrooms to support the demonstration. Such coercion appears to have been limited and was not condoned by the leadership. The Action Committee's lack of experience and limited resources meant that its political authority was strongest where it was physically present. Beyond this central core, there was considerable fragmentation of effort and activity. Nonetheless, the deep antipathy towards the government's language policy and growing discontent about the poor state of African education brought thousands of students behind the banner of the Action Committee.

Students on the march
Police reports of events on the morning of 16 June provide some insight into how the marches from different schools unfolded:

08h00: Students meet at Naledi High School. Tebello Motapanyane leads them to Orlando West High. Passing Thomas Mofolo and Morris

Isaacson students join in. Morris Isaacson students march to Thesele High in White City. Students force motorists to give the 'Black Power' salute.

08h10: A school inspector in a car is attacked by marching students. Colonel J.J. Gerber, divisional commander of Soweto police, investigates conditions in Naledi. He reports to Brigadier Le Roux that 800 to 1000 students are marching to Orlando, attacking cars and stoning police. He finds that there are too few policemen at Jabulani police station to disperse the students. Brigadier Le Roux learns from other station commanders that many youths are assembling, overturning cars and setting them alight. He orders them to mobilise all available policemen and to restrict students to school grounds.

08h20: Another 600 students join the 900 marching from Naledi to Orlando. Major G.J. Viljoen, station commander at Jabulani, tells West Rand Administration Board officials and other whites to leave the area. Those marching to Orlando West High are joined by others. A procession in the direction of Orlando West High is followed by Colonel Kleingeld and two sergeants. When the students notice the police, they begin throwing stones. Colonel Kleingeld returns for reinforcements and issues guns to the officers.

09h15: Two journalists, one black and one white, arrive at the Phefeni Junior Secondary School. Teachers warn them to leave the area because of the approach of the Naledi High students. The white journalist is threatened and leaves.

09h30: A black crowd greets a white journalist with 'Black Power' salutes at the Orlando police station. He senses the atmosphere is tense.

This stream of reports from police came to form the foundation of 'facts' upon which the official narrative of events was constructed. Central to this version was the deliberate attempt to portray students as unruly and undisciplined, and as the instigators of violence from the time they left the schools. The police claimed to have come under attack and that they merely responded to rising tensions and further threats of violence. However, this rendition of the 'facts' stands in direct contrast to the testimonies of student participants and other witnesses.

According to Murphy Morobe, the Action Committee meeting held on Monday 14 June drafted clear plans for the marches, whose implementation was to be co-ordinated by senior activists. Schools were divided into 'three streams', each led by students from one of the three main high schools involved in the Action Committee, namely, Morris Isaacson, Naledi and Sekano Ntoane. The basic plan was for marchers to proceed from here, collect students from other schools and head for a central meeting point. Although there are different recollections about the precise routes and destination, there is general agreement that students were asked to march past Phefeni Junior Secondary as a show of solidarity with the school at the centre of the boycott and then congregate in Orlando West. One version of the plan seems to have been that all students would gather at Orlando Stadium and then proceed to the regional offices of the Department of Bantu Education in Booysens to hand over a memorandum of grievances. Morobe, who was a central figure in the planning of the demonstration, has said that the plan 'was just to get to Orlando West, pledge our solidarity … have a mass rally, where the student leaders, Tsietsi Mashinini and them, would be able to address the students … sing "Nkosi Sikelel' iAfrika" … and thereafter in fact break off the march. Then we thought we would have made our point and we would go back home.' At that stage, student leaders did not know what to expect from the authorities and, according to Morobe, could do no more than agree 'to look towards the situation where we could anticipate and expect a response from the authorities in terms of our demands … And the idea was that subsequent to that we are going to.'

The Action Committee had also decided that its members would lead the three main contingents. Tsietsi Mashinini, Lazarus Mphahlele and Murphy Morobe were charged with the responsibility of heading the march from Morris Isaacson. From there they proceeded to the suburb of Mofolo, where they mobilised students from Thesele Junior Secondary School. Tebello Motapanyane and David Kutumela led the demonstration from Naledi Senior Secondary School. This second stream collected students from Thomas Mofolo Junior Secondary and Moletsane Junior Secondary. Dan Mofokeng was part of this group and remembers marching from Thomas Mofolo to various other schools: 'There was also Batswana Junior Secondary ... We were collecting other junior secondary schools, Tladi, Moletsane, right through around Phefeni station.' The final contingent proceeded from Sekano Ntoane Senior Secondary School, collected students from Senaoane Junior Secondary School and then marched to Potchefstroom Road. According to George Baloyi, this final group split up after reaching the main road: 'we went out and it was ordered that some other should go here, and some other should go there. Therefore we went down straight and met at Regina Mundi [church] ... There were new leaders now.' Apart from lacking a focused leadership, those who headed for Potchefstroom Road were very late in meeting the rest of the marchers in Orlando West.

Colin Nxumalo, a resident of Orlando West, was a traffic officer at the time and was on duty on the Moroka Nancefield Road. His description of the marchers as they approached one of the township's busiest intersections highlights the co-operation between students and officials like him, as well as the students' discipline. 'In the morning we saw a group of school children, they were coming from that side of cross-roads, coming towards us, we were standing at the intersection, at Mncube and Nancefield. They were coming down Moroka Nancefield Road. As they were coming, they closed the road and filled the street, so we went to them trying to control the traffic, because it was still in the morning, and taxis were on the road going to the Nancefield station. We tried to control traffic and also to ensure that they are safe … They then came to the intersection, Mncube Drive.' From here Nxumalo and a colleague, Fraser Ramokgopa, accompanied the students into Orlando West, where they met students coming from other parts of the township. Contrary to police reports, the marchers were well organised and disciplined, determined to deliver a united and powerful message to the authorities by congregating in Orlando West. The mood was charged and highly political. But there was also an air of exuberance and celebration. Dan Moyane has captured the prevailing spirit among the students: 'We were singing and it was jovial, the mood, exciting, and with the placards we started going, we started going. We went and went. We passed Mofolo, other people were joining us as we were going along, other kids, and everybody was in school uniform, everyone … we were nicely going and there was nothing, nothing tense.'

Simon Ramapepe described the marchers as 'just a mob of happy students marching and chanting. If they could have just left us alone we would have chanted and chanted and got tired, and gone back home at the end of the day.' One of George Baloyi's main memories of that morning was that 'There was a lot of singing then. We did not know the songs, we were hearing them for the first time.' At that time the repertoire of freedom songs was quite limited, with political songs often being interspersed with popular hymns. The peaceful and rhetorical 'Senzenina?' (What have we done?) and the anthem 'Nkosi Sikelel' iAfrika' were the most popular songs on the day. More potently, shouts of 'Black Power!' filled the air and became the signature slogan of the uprising. But it was the handmade posters that captured the main grievances of the thousands of students marching through the streets of Soweto:

> To Hell with Afrikaans!
> Away with Afrikaans!
> Down with Bantu Education!
> Afrikaans pollutes our minds!
> Afrikaans retards our progress!
> Afrikaans means confined to S. Africa!

What had started as a series of isolated protests at the beginning of 1976 was now transformed into an unprecedented mass movement, united behind a single demand: to hell with Afrikaans! This unity of purpose was reflected, first of all, in the solidarity expressed by students from across Soweto with the protest at Phefeni Junior Secondary and, secondly, in the congregation of thousands of students in the streets of Orlando West around 10 am. When students reached Orlando High School, they were addressed by one of the student leaders. Sophie Tema, a journalist, remembers his appeal to the thousands of students gathered at that point: 'Brothers and sisters, I appeal to you to keep calm and cool. We have just received a report that the police are coming. Please do not taunt them, do not do anything to them, just be cool and calm because we do not know what they are after. We are not fighting.'

But the arrival of the police completely changed the dynamics of the situation. According to Morobe, 'No one envisaged a process that would go beyond June 16th. Little did we expect the kind of reaction that we got from the police on that day.' Ramapepe is even more pointed about the culpability of the police: 'Actually, if I could tell you about this day, the law or the police made a mess of everything.'

The police shoot to kill

It is worth noting the historic significance of the mass march through the streets of Soweto. Although there were demonstrations in the late 1950s and early 1960s, especially against passes, Soweto had not experienced such a large and co-ordinated demonstration by students in its entire history. The protest on 16 June was crucial because, among other things, it challenged at least two cornerstones of the apartheid state's control over black lives. The first, obviously, was Bantu Education. The second, though it is much less acknowledged, was the challenge to the state's control over the lived spaces of black people. By the 1960s the state had met one of its key objectives, first espoused in the early 1950s, of entrenching 'model and modern' African townships as spaces of order and control. It managed to assert tight control over townships such as Soweto through various technologies of surveillance and means of coercion – passes, permits, threats of deportation to poor rural areas, housing, 'blackjacks', white township officials, black councillors and so forth. This spatial control was an important factor behind the political quiescence in the post-Sharpeville period.

In early 1976 student demonstrations against Afrikaans were confined to school grounds and were dealt with as localised incidents by the authorities, even when confrontations between the police and students became more heated. But the Action Committee's decision to organise a mass march marked a qualitative shift in the character of township protest. By taking to the streets, students directly challenged the state's control over the township and, as the conflict with the police intensified, vociferously claimed the streets as belonging to them, the black residents of Soweto. From the perspective of the state, the demonstration posed a threat to the essential elements of its machinery of control and therefore had to be crushed.

Evidence at the Cillie Commission revealed that the police had been forewarned about the planned march, but failed to take preparatory steps. As a result, they frantically mobilised their forces at the same time as students began to congregate at their schools. All police in Soweto were placed on full alert at 7 am and over the next few hours they collected information about the unfolding demonstration. Led by the infamous Colonel J.A. Kleingeld, the police then moved to confront the students, determined to halt the peaceful protest. According to police reports, the first skirmish with students took place at 10 am. 'Police are stoned by about 600 students when they arrive at the Tshabalala garage. Teargas does not deter them. Another 600 students join the group. The police are withdrawn as they are too few to cope with the situation.' According to Colin Nxumalo, the police also tried to stop the march at Mncube. 'Then as we were at the corner, there came 41 hundred [a Chevrolet 4100] the other one is cream white and the other one is green. I never forget that. When they came, those Chevs 41 hundred, we know them after all, that they are the security cars. They then started shooting teargas … They started at Mncube and Moroka Nancefield, they started there to pour teargas.' Most students had never experienced teargas. According to Erick Ngobeni: 'It was the first day to taste it. I didn't know that it was teargas. As you know, we grew up without knowing that such things are used. I first thought that it might be a light mist that happened to occur just along the road. It surprised me, because it troubled my eyes a little, you see, even my nose. We were breathing in an unusual way.'

Despite these efforts by the police, the marchers continued along the routes set out by the leadership. From around 10 am, students were streaming from different directions into Orlando West. Mrs Sithole, a long-time resident of Orlando West, watched the students as they marched down the road: 'Yes! I said: "This is now serious" and they're now at school and now they came down, now they were singing. As I went out, I saw police at the corner at the robot, you see the robots … So, they were standing there, I said to myself: "No! They won't do anything." The children came, and they came down this way, coming down thousands … thousands of them, thousands all schools uniform. They had nothing, they were not aggressive. They were just having placards saying: "Away with Afrikaans".'

Once the students reached Orlando West, the situation changed dramatically when the police used violence to stop the march. Kleingeld was the commanding officer in charge of Orlando and in his testimony to the Cillie Commission he claimed that he issued several warnings to the students to disperse. But the Commission's final report cast some doubt on his version and concluded that he did not give 'the riotous crowd an audible and effective order to disperse and depart from the place'. Sophie Tema expressed surprise about the police's failure to use a loudspeaker to address the protesters, who were singing and thus unlikely to hear instructions. A reporter on the *Rand Daily Mail* wrote the following day: 'I did not hear the police give any order to disperse before they threw teargas canisters into the crowd of singing students.' In fact the police report of the minutes leading up to the shooting of Hector Pieterson revealed a deliberate effort to blame the students for attacking them first. '10h30: Several thousand students gather around a koppie at Orlando West High. Colonel Kleingeld's party is stoned and he cannot address the crowd. Four blacks are inciting the students. Teargas and a baton charge are ineffective. Police are attacked and some are hit by stones. Colonel Kleingeld fires five pistol shots over the crowd with no effect. He then fires 20 shots with an automatic rifle in front of and over the crowd. Others fire shots with their revolvers and pistols although Colonel Kleingeld did not give the order to fire. A black youth, Hector Pieterson, is fatally wounded by the police. A female reporter takes his body to the Phomolong Clinic.'

But other witness testimonies completely contradicted the police's version of events. Sophie Tema was one of a handful of journalists who followed the march from early in the morning and was present when the police opened fire. Her recollection of the sequence of events submitted to the Commission of Inquiry debunked the police's claims of acting in self-defence: 'The police first threw teargas into the midst of the students. Then some of the students in the front line hurled stones at them in retaliation, it was then that this policeman pulled out the revolver, aimed at the students and fired. It was after this policeman had fired and more shots followed, that most of the students attacked the police.' This version of the tragic events is supported by Mrs Sithole, who witnessed the unfolding confrontation from the front of her house. What happened next, she recalled, 'is still embedded in my mind'. 'When the police came … I was outside watching. Now I'm worried "where are these kids?", because now I can see that the police vans and everything. When they were just near here the police came and they talked, they chat saying to them "go back to school" and children said "NO!" They were against Afrikaans. They did not have stones, they didn't have anything! Whoever said the children had anything like stones … It's not so, it's a lie … the police just opened fire. There were little children coming from this side. They came from this street. I remember their uniform was green and grey. They came from this side and the police opened fire! And all hell broke loose here. And the little boy fell here between these two houses, between my house and here.'

The police shot indiscriminately into the mass of students. By all accounts the teargas sowed panic among the students. Some ran away to escape, while others quickly learned how to overcome the effects or else threw the canisters back. Still others stood firm and confronted the police. 'There was pandemonium' is how Morobe describes what happened after the police shot into the crowd of students.

Hastings Ndlovu was shot and killed around the same time as Hector Pieterson. Their deaths came to symbolise the violence of the apartheid state. Hastings was leading a group of students who intended to march from Orlando West Junior Secondary to Orlando Stadium. They were confronted by police at the Orlando West bridge, where Hastings was reportedly shot at close range by Colonel Kleingeld. At about the same time Hector Pieterson was also killed. The photograph taken by Sam Nzima of Mbuyisa Makhubo carrying Hector's lifeless body, with Antoinette Sithole (Hector's sister) running alongside, has become the iconic moment and image of the 1976 uprising. Antoinette has vividly recounted the frightening minutes before she realised her younger brother had been shot: 'As we came out from hiding, I was scared and I said: "It seems this is going to go on and on. So what can one do?" I was thinking very hard and I forgot about Hector … We came on foot. That's another problem. Even if you want to go home, how are you going to go home? So I was thinking about that … I looked around, … thinking maybe he's still hiding. He's small. Maybe he's still hiding, he's still frightened … I told myself that I'm not going to move from that place. He might come looking for me. Let me stay here. While I was there, thinking about that, I could see a group of boys, about three or four, at a distance … They were struggling and other students who were hanging around on the pavement were going to that scene … I want to go there but I don't know how because I'm thinking of Hector that he might look for me and not find me … I was very scared. It's almost about seven minutes and Hector hasn't come out. My heart was beating so fast but I tried to get hold of myself. As they came closer, the gentleman … whom I knew later [as] Mbuyisa Makhubo, … lifted … a body and, as he lifted it higher, the first thing that I saw was the front part of Hector's shoe. Then I said: "Those shoes belong to Hector!" I just said that and I just went to the scene. Mbuyisa was already running. And on the way when we were running I asked him: "Who are you? This is my brother. I've been looking for him." I didn't know how to explain myself.'

These killings signalled a sharp turning point in the confrontation between students and the police, and inaugurated a new phase in young black people's role in the broader struggle against apartheid. On the day, they instantly transformed a peaceful protest into a riot that was to leave deep scars on Soweto.

The riot
News of the killing of Hector Pieterson and Hastings Ndlovu spread like wildfire through the ranks of the protesters, generating fear, panic and, mostly, deep anger. At the scene of the shooting, Tsietsi Mashinini briefly

addressed the crowd and attempted to maintain some control over events. 'Our intention was to go to Orlando Stadium, and hold the mass meeting there,' he reminded his increasingly restless audience, 'but since there have been disruptions, it seems that we have to disperse.' However, the police attacks made it virtually impossible to achieve an orderly return to homes and schools. Instead, as Morobe has observed, there was an 'angry and volatile retreat'. Events now unfolded at break-neck speed as students fled the scene in all directions, with the police in pursuit. Within a short period of time many sections of the township were transformed into a battlefield.

The ensuing riot produced two notable shifts in the political contestation between students and the state. First, the streets became the main battleground between the contending forces, with both sides seemingly aware that control over those spaces would be crucial in determining the outcome of the violent political contest. Second, the police's violent response to the peaceful march not only triggered the ensuing riot, but also contributed to a dramatic shift in the political consciousness of large sections of the students. At the start of the day students had set out to express their objections to Afrikaans. By the end of the day many had drawn the conclusion that the battle to be engaged was now against the apartheid system as a whole. Solly Mpshe was part of the demonstration in Orlando West and also fled the scene after the shooting. It was then, he recalls, that his political awareness changed fundamentally: 'People started moving out of the area. And if they came across anything that could be associated with the system, [it] was targeted. That afternoon I learnt the popular word: "the system". So, on our way back, anything that was associated with "the system" was stoned and we managed to put our hand on anything to take home.'

When he saw Sam Nzima's image of the dying Hector Pieterson in the paper the following day, Mpshe was overcome with anger. 'I think that is the picture that made me to be angry and hate the system.' Tulu Mhlanga was similarly affected by the photograph. Initially, he says, 'It frightened me a lot because Hector Pieterson was younger than me. So imagine seeing a young child shot. I was feeling bad.' But like many of his peers, Tulu's reaction to police violence was not to retreat or submit. On the contrary he was emboldened. 'The event', he has proudly declared, 'made me so strong and [I] got deep in the struggle.'

Witnessing shootings and deaths engendered a new-found courage among many young people: the courage not only to confront superior armed forces but, crucially, a willingness to die for the cause. Gandhi Mlungane epitomised this mood: 'it made me to feel like fighting until I die, because I saw people dying next to me and in front of me. On the 17th, 18th, I saw people dying, but I couldn't give up, because we were prepared to die, like the song said: "When we die, we go forward".' This turn marked a sea-change in black politics. For the first time since the late 1950s the apartheid government was confronted by a mass movement, now overwhelmingly youthful and increasingly militant. Critically, these new battalions of the anti-apartheid movement were not afraid to stand up to the well-armed security forces. An increasing number of them were prepared to die for the cause.

Police reinforcements streamed into the township to put down the rebellion. Victor Buthelezi remembers that 'soldiers were moving all over the area'. Initially, fear gripped the township and students were advised not to congregate together or even walk in groups, to avoid attacks by the police. 'It was dangerous for everybody and we hid ourselves,' says Buthelezi, but 'when they pass we were running all over the area.' While some students returned to the safety of their homes, many others engaged in running battles with police. Sam Zikhali joined a group involved in continuous skirmishes with the police. He explains: 'Every group [was] moving down, up and down, and policemen were shooting. Some of the guys were injured, some were drunk. Right, right up until past twelve, one o'clock the following morning, it was the same thing. We went to Orlando, dodging these policemen, throwing stones.'

Students vented their anger primarily at the police, who were the most visible and violent agents of the state. But their hatred of 'the system' also extended to other symbols and representatives of apartheid in the township. Foremost among these were the offices and officials of the West Rand Administration Board (WRAB). Administration Boards were established in the early 1970s to centralise the administration of African townships. Until then, white municipalities had run the affairs of the African areas in their jurisdiction, a system which the National Party deemed too fragmented and unreliable. To ensure its ideological mission would be dutifully pursued, the government took direct control over the administration of Africans' lives. A network of surveillance and control was created in townships, at the centre of which stood the Administration Board offices, run by white officials. It was from these offices that various aspects of African people's lives were managed: this was where residential permits were issued, where youths applied for job permits, where raids were organised to uncover and deport 'illegal' residents, and houses were allocated.

Dan Moyane describes how the group he joined attacked one of the WRAB offices on their way from Orlando West. 'I went [with] a group of guys. We jumped because then the [municipal] offices were closed – most of the superintendents were white and they were gone. So we jumped in there, guys broke in the doors and everything else, and then petrol … petrol was now freely available and petrol-bombing started, everything was burnt.' These buildings were deemed to be legitimate

Burnt-out offices of the WRAB.

targets because they were regarded as part of the white state apparatus. Solomon Marikele explained what he thought were legitimate targets: 'The following day I pick up stones. I joined the struggle. I did whatever we were supposed to do during [those] days, because we were burning everything, offices, you know, municipal offices mostly. Breaking schools, burning cars from the white man. As long as that thing belonged to a white man, we burn it.'

Sam Zikhali came to a similar conclusion during the course of the day. Ironically, his school, Ibhongo Junior Senior Secondary, was writing examinations when the protesters marched to Orlando West. At about 11am, Zikhali and his schoolmates witnessed fighting between

A Soweto bottlestore destroyed by fire.

protesting students and police in the street. He remembers them becoming very angry when they heard that white policemen had shot black students. At that point they decided to join the fight because 'we all hated the white people'. In the aftermath of the shooting in Orlando West, this anger towards white people became widespread. A few minutes after the first shots were fired some protesting students stoned a car with four white female occupants, who managed to flee from the township. At about the same time another group of students encountered Mr J.N.B. Esterhuizen, a WRAB official, in Khumalo Street. Unlike the women in the car, Esterhuizen did not escape the wrath of the students and was beaten to death. The same fate befell the social worker Dr Melville Edelstein, who was caught in one of the WRAB offices.

Beerhalls were also regarded as an important part of the state's apparatus of control, especially of African men, large numbers of whom spent their meagre wages on the consumption of traditional beer. Because the government owned the beerhalls, it had a monopoly over the production and sale of traditional beer in townships. Profits from beer sales constituted a vital revenue stream for the financing of the township administrations. Students were especially perturbed by the contribution of alcohol abuse to the political quiescence of adults. The destruction of beerhalls was thus intended to send a strong message to both the authorities and adults. Bottlestores were attacked for similar reasons. But, as Vusi Zwane explains, the attacks on bottlestores marked the entry of non-students to the violence. 'The 16th was one of those days I have never seen in the whole world because it was smoke all over. Then those old people who took advantage and went to work. Some were breaking in the bottlestores and stole liquor. Beers. It was noise all over, noise throughout the night.'

Unemployed youth, especially *tsotsis*, now took advantage of the chaos prevailing in some parts of the township to loot bottlestores and other shops. While some *tsotsis* were caught up in the explosion of political protests and allied themselves with the political objectives of the student movement, many saw an opportunity to pursue their criminal activities. As they were not under any form of political discipline, tensions arose between *tsotsis* and students. Over the next few months the ill-discipline of *tsotsis* became an acute problem which the student leadership struggled to contain.

Protests continued late into night of the 16th. In fact, the township hardly paused for breath. A few minutes after midnight, reports came in of the WRAB offices in Meadowlands being set alight. The police responded by firing bullets and teargas into the assembled crowd. Over the following 24 hours similar scenes were repeated all over Soweto. From early in the morning groups of protesters, ranging from a handful to as many as 3000, gathered to confront the presence of the police and continue the destruction of official buildings. By mid-morning the township again resembled a war zone, with large numbers of police in armed vehicles patrolling the streets, continuous battles between protesters and police, numerous buildings on fire, and the number of injured and dead rising steadily throughout the day. Again, the Cillie Commission report provided an almost blow-by-blow account of the traumatic events that unfolded on the morning of 17 June:

7h00: The WRAB offices for Areas 2 and 3, Meadowlands, were set on fire.
7h30: A WRAB sanitary depot in Area 2, Meadowlands, was set on fire. The Police arrested a number of people.

7h50: After a beer hall in area had been destroyed, about 3000 rioters attacked the Naledi Railway Station … Four bodies with gunshot wounds were found by the police in the veld near the Naledi Railway Station. Four bodies were found in the veld at Zondi.

8h30: A large crowd of about 1300 persons was milling around in Masepha Street, Orlando East. Youths in school uniform were among those present. The crowd attacked the police with stones and the police used firearms and teargas.

9h10: The police shot dead two persons in a stone-throwing crowd at the WRAB office in Diepkloof.

The image etched in Hendrick Tshabalala's memory is that on the 17th 'the whole of Soweto was in flames, cars and many things were burning'. He has given interesting insights into the character of the violence on that day: 'The police and soldiers were now shooting indiscriminately. People were stoning the police and running at the same time, the same was happening to the police and the soldiers. Something I found to be surprising was the police attacked every child, whether he was causing havoc or not. The children were also attacking cars whether they belonged to the whites or not.'

Though battle lines were drawn all over Soweto, the streets became the primary sites of contestation. Potchefstroom Road, one of the main arterial routes running through the township and a key link between it and the city of Johannesburg, became a central focus of protest. Hendrick Tshabalala was among the many students 'who were going to Potchefstroom [Road], the place where everything was happening'. There was little, if any, pre-planning: 'There was no meeting. We meet there on the Potchefstroom [Road], then we started the action from there. There is no meeting, there is nothing. We throw stones when we see the white man's car is coming. Whatever we break, we burn.' Such demonstrations on a main road gave greater visibility to the protests, which further heightened the struggle for control over this space.

Rumours, fed by fears of vengeful police acting with impunity against all young people, quickly spread across the township. One of these was that police snipers were driving around in unmarked cars. Steve Lebelo explains: 'I do know that suddenly there was the infamous green car. It was a 3800 Chev [Chevrolet], it was a green car, and at that time they were mostly used by police. We suspected that they had a sniper in there, who picked up people at random and shot and killed them.' Fear was certainly pervasive among young people, who were the main targets of the police. In some areas, the police went from house to house, and, according to Vusi Zwane, they were especially 'searching for boys, for any boys. That thing forced us to run away from our homes. We went to sleep in schools because they came to our homes.'

Martha Matthews remarked: 'The following day it was worse because these boers were now following people inside their yards. We could not go out. We could not go buy in shops. There was no person who [was] walking on the streets. It was bad, bad … I'm telling [you], if you want to die, just get outside the house. Even if you are not doing anything, they would shoot you.' After a few days nearly 150 vehicles and about 140 buildings had been burned. Violence continued for several months and it was estimated that after three months nearly 300 black youths and adults were killed and more than 2000 injured.

Black Parents' Association
It was students who led every aspect of the uprising, from the conceptualisation of the protest to confronting state violence. Adults were only peripheral to these events. This marginal role has been attributed to their supposed political conservatism and fear. These were undoubtedly important issues but they only partially explain their initial lack of involvement. Another contributing factor was the absence of progressive township-based organisations that could mobilise adults. There was as yet no equivalent among parents of organisations such as SASM, NAYO or SASO.

As the crisis surrounding Afrikaans intensified in 1976, some parents did start to make efforts to organise themselves. The most notable of these initiatives occurred in early June, when Dr Aaron Matlhare, a medical doctor practising in Soweto, convened a public meeting at Naledi Hall, attended by approximately 300 residents. The aim of the meeting was to create a parents' association that would address the multiple problems facing Soweto residents. Winnie Mandela, who was widely regarded as a leading activist in the township, addressed the meeting and gave it her enthusiastic support. An interim executive committee was nominated, with Matlhare as the chairman and Mandela serving as a committee member. The primary task of the new committee was to convene an inaugural conference of the new organisation at the end of June, a plan that was, however, overtaken by the student uprising.

On the evening of 17 June, members of the interim executive of the Parents' Association, leaders of the BPC and student leaders met to discuss the crisis. Present were Kenneth Hlaku Rachidi and Tom Manthatha (BPC), Aubrey Mokoena (Black Community Programmes), Winnie Mandela, Aaron Matlhare and Dr Nthato Motlana, as well as the students leaders Tsietsi Mashinini, Seth Mazibuko, Zweli Sizani and Tebello Motapanyane. The meeting was held at the Revd Desmond Tutu's residence, a few houses down the road from the Mandela home. It was an attempt to establish a working relationship between the student leadership and those adults regarded as generally supportive of the students' struggles. However, the gathering got off to a tense start when the students questioned the commitment of some of the adults, nearly causing a rift at the outset.

Fortunately, cooler heads prevailed and agreement was quickly reached on basic co-operation. A joint public statement condemning police violence was drafted and plans were made to convene a more representative meeting to discuss arrangements for the funerals of those killed in the violence. The following evening a bigger meeting was convened at the Methodist Church in Central Jabavu West. Representatives from a wide range of organisations were present, including the Soweto Parents' Association, SASM, SASO, BPC and BCP. Following a suggestion by Dr Motlana, it was agreed to replace the SPA with the Black Parents' Association (BPA), because the former was deemed to have too narrow a geographical scope. At the same time it was argued the new organisation should aim to draw in black parents from townships beyond Soweto. Manas Buthelezi, from the Lutheran Church, was elected chairman and Matlhare his deputy. The BPA's immediate responsibility was to support bereaved families and to organise a mass funeral at the end of June.

Tension between students and the adult leadership resurfaced when the government banned the planned mass funeral. While students called for defiance of the banning order, the chairman of the BPA was prepared to accede to the order and arrange individual funerals for each of the victims. After heated debate a compromise was reached whereby Hector Pieterson's funeral, which was held on 3 July, would be organised as *the* symbolic mass funeral. Despite disagreements a provisional alliance had been struck between students and a section of parents. The BPA did not initially have a large following or organisational base in the township but its leadership did enjoy respect among significant sections of the adult population. Their support of the students' struggle established an important bridge between the two constituencies, which would prove crucial in the months following the June rebellion.

5

The aftermath
Shaping a new mass movement

After the intense conflict of mid-June, Soweto paused to make sense of the historic events that had engulfed it. A 'volatile lull' prevailed between mid-June and the end of July. The extended closure of schools and the ubiquitous presence of large numbers of police, who relentlessly harassed the youth, especially those identified as leaders, seriously curtailed the Action Committee's efforts to continue mobilising students. As a result, many students retreated into inactivity. However, some groups of students and youth continued to engage the security forces on the streets, albeit increasingly intermittently and on a smaller scale than at the height of the battles in mid-June. Another crucial problem confronting the student leadership was the infiltration of protests by *tsotsis*, who took advantage of the situation to loot stores and even rob people. By mid-July it became apparent that the struggle launched the previous month was in danger of foundering under the twin threat of state repression and *tsotsi* ill-discipline. Parents and many students were alienated by what they perceived as a growing tendency of lawlessness and expressed concern about the future of education in the township. Meeting these challenges became a primary preoccupation of the Action Committee and SASM, and from late July they began to act decisively to regain leadership of the students' movement.

The eruption of mass protests and the state's violent response had shattered the post-Sharpeville quiescence. On 6 July the government abandoned its Afrikaans medium policy, which represented an historic victory for the students of Soweto. As a result, the initial focus of the student movement disappeared. What followed was a process of configuring a new politics of struggle against apartheid, in which students and youth played a central role. This was uncharted territory for the nascent mass movement of students and their allies. There were many challenges, including the inexperience of student leaders, organisational weakness, state repression and the use of conservative political forces to divide the community. Parents were generally supportive but also fearful. Nonetheless, what shone through during this period was the élan of youth and a steely determination to advance the struggle against apartheid.

These were seminal processes in the reconfiguration of liberation politics, in which students were the leading actors. At the beginning of the year, most of those who later constituted the leadership of the uprising had very little, if any, experience of actual political struggles.

Their political ideas were generally better developed, especially those involved in SASM and various informal political groups. After 16 June, amidst intense political conflict, leaders of the movement quickly acquired organisational skills, and were compelled to formulate tactics and strategies, analyse the fluid political situation and respond to myriad challenges. In the process, they combined their enthusiasm and courage with increasing political sophistication, albeit unevenly and not without error. Meetings of the Soweto Students' Representative Council (SSRC), with up to a hundred representatives in attendance, were regularly convened to receive report-backs and discuss the unfolding political situation in the township as well as nationally. Students had to navigate a minefield of contentious issues, including examinations, the return to school, the presence of *tsotsis*, and the need for creating alliances with parents and workers and with other progressive organisations, while also having to demonstrate leadership of the mounting struggle against 'the system'. Pamphlets articulating the views, programmes and plans of action of the SSRC were regularly disseminated throughout the township. The ability of the newly created SSRC to lead the struggle in Soweto was seriously tested in the latter half of 1976, particularly as the state intensified its repression.

SSRC takes the lead
Schools were supposed to reopen on 15 July, but the

state feared further mobilisation and sought first to assert control over the situation in Soweto, banning all meetings from 16 July. Furthermore, the amended Internal Security Act was immediately brought into effect, giving the police legal authority to detain people for an indefinite period without trial. At a meeting on 26 July, school principals and teachers expressed their deep concern about the presence of large contingents of armed forces in the township and appealed 'for the removal of "hippos" [armoured police cars] from the vicinity of schools, as they were frightening the pupils'.

Believing it had regained some control in the township, the state announced that schools in Soweto would reopen on 22 July. This triggered a debate among students over whether to return to school. Most leaders of the Action Committee called for a return because, first of all, they wanted teaching to be resumed. Secondly, it was proving extremely difficult to mobilise students while they were dispersed at home throughout the township. Schools provided pivotal bases for student organisation and had enabled the Action Committee to assert a degree of political leadership over the mass of students. Most parents also supported the call for a return to school. However, a significant proportion of students opposed the Action Committee's position. In their view, education had been irretrievably disrupted for the year. They pointed to the abandonment of the mid-year examinations and persistent police repression as major justifications for supporting a protracted school boycott. As a result, there was a mixed response to the official reopening. In fact, police raids on schools in the first few weeks of the new term effectively caused a resumption of the school boycott.

The uncertainty surrounding the resumption of schooling highlighted the lack of cohesion in the student movement. Both parents and student leaders took steps to remedy this situation. On 1 August, the Black Parents' Association (BPA) convened a meeting at Regina Mundi church to discuss the ongoing crisis in the schools. Tsietsi Mashinini addressed the meeting and again appealed to students to return to the classroom. At the same time the Action Committee and SASM were preparing to call a meeting of all schools in the township. On 2 August the emergency meeting, attended by 40 student delegates, was held at Morris Isaacson. It reiterated the position adopted by the Action Committee, condemning the burning of schools and endorsing the call to resume classes. Attendees also criticised the Urban Bantu Council of Soweto, labelling it a 'stooge body'. After intense deliberations, the meeting drafted a memorandum of demands, which the BPA was entrusted with submitting to the authorities on behalf of the students.

Perhaps the most important resolution adopted by the gathering was to establish the Soweto Students' Representative Council. According to Sibongile Mkhabela, SASM played a key role because it 'felt that more co-ordination was necessary'. SASM, she explains, 'set about it in this way: two representatives of each school in Soweto were nominated to an umbrella body'. Tsietsi Mashinini, whose charismatic leadership of the Action Committee made him an instant hero of the struggle in Soweto, was elected as chairman. The reinvigorated student leadership eagerly set about mobilising the Soweto community. As the most representative co-ordinating structure, the SSRC effectively assumed the leadership of its student constituency. For example, in order to deal directly with the problem of *tsotsis*, it resolved to establish 'squads' with the aim of disciplining unruly youth gangs and to offer protection to residents against them. Its success in this regard is unclear, but the decision to act against *tsotsis* undoubtedly won it widespread kudos in the township. A few days after the launch, Mashinini issued a memorandum on behalf of the SSRC, which clearly set out the main grievances of the students:

WE, the SSRC condemn:

1. Police action in Soweto by irresponsibly shooting at students on their way to school or black children playing in the location as it has been reported in the newspapers. We see it as an unofficial declaration of war on black students by our 'peace-officers'.

2. The statement by Mr Gert Prinsloo [Soweto police commissioner] that the racist regime will

not succumb to the demands of a 'handful of students' instead we are the voice of the people and our demands shall be met.

3. The response by Jimmy Kruger [Minister of Justice and Police] that he not will accept the BPA as the authentic body representing us. We see no peace and order if our demands are not met.

4. The statement by the Prime Minister that the racist regime 'will not panic'. We do not anticipate panic but expect responsible ACTION from the leaders of this country.

5. The action of elements burning schools we believe that is no black man's action.

6. The brutality experienced by students in police hands especially those who have been recently arrested and released.

7. The abuse of power by security officers to refuse relatives to see detainees and demand a just investigation in the suspicious conditions in which Mr Mapetla Mohapi [secretary of SASO] died [on 5 August] and we are afraid the same may befall our people detained in connection with the so called 'riots'.

8. I, Tsietsi Mashinini, appeal to students to report back to school and notify the authorities of any injured dead or missing students. We still have our end exams to write and we must have our

priorities sorted.

9. WE lastly condemn the detention of BPA members and see it as an unwarranted move by the system. We never meant them to meet Mr Kruger in detention.

Ours is a peaceful struggle which only the racist regime can curb by a dialogue with our leaders.

Mashinini's statement marked the fact that the launch of the SSRC had opened a new phase in the students' struggle. Confrontations between students and police had reached a stalemate, while the state's harassment, detention and killings continued unabated. Challenging state repression thus became a central focus for the SSRC. At the same time the SSRC aimed to overcome the fragmentation that the movement had suffered during the closure of the schools. Politically, the student leadership had now broadened its critique to include Bantu Education and the whole apartheid system. The SSRC quickly established itself as the leading organisation of students and of the struggle in Soweto. It demanded as a result that the state recognise it and the BPA as the legitimate representatives of the people in the township.

There seems to have been an implicit acknowledgement by the SSRC of the limitations of township-bound student struggles and thus of the need to formulate new strategies to advance the broad struggle against apartheid and specifically to pressure the state to accede to its immediate demands. Political activists decided it was necessary to strike blows at the heart of white power if there was to be any prospect of obtaining concessions. Strikes by black workers, they concluded, would hit the economy hard and force the state, employers and white society in general to listen to the demands of black people. Interestingly, pamphlets issued by the African National Congress (ANC) in the aftermath of the June uprising echoed this assessment. One such pamphlet urged students to advance the struggle against apartheid by transcending the bounds of the township: 'Because the protests were largely confined to the locations, damage to the economy, the heart of white power, was limited – the struggle must be taken into the cities, the factories, the mines.'

Interviewed in exile, Mashinini later denied that the SSRC's new strategy had been determined by the ANC. The students had, however, drawn inspiration from the mass struggles of the 1940s and 1950s when work stayaways were periodically organised by communities and political organisations. *Azikhwelwa!* (We won't ride) became the rallying slogan in those struggles, and was especially used to great effect during the Alexandra bus boycotts during those two decades. In 1976, intense discussion took place between student and adult activists, many of whom were adherents of Black Consciousness and probably also included supporters of the ANC.

But while members of BCM, BPA and others were also involved, SASM appears to have played the leading role in shaping the politics of the students' movement. The strategies and tactics of the students in 1976 evolved from within this movement, rather than being determined by external political organisations.

Mkhabela has provided a succinct explanation of the political rationale behind the SSRC's and SASM's new tactic: 'In order to hit the economy, we appealed to our working and toiling masses to join students in an assault on the "system", in this instance the captains of industry and a government which enabled them to accumulate ill-gotten wealth at the expense of our parents – the slave wage earners.' This now became the main focus of the SSRC. It created unprecedented potential for establishing an alliance between students and workers, but simultaneously presented a serious challenge for the relations between different generations in the township.

Azikhwelwa – We won't ride!

The most important campaign launched by the SSRC was a call for the immediate release of all students detained by the police. It was decided at the founding meeting to organise a march to the police headquarters in Johannesburg in pursuit of this objective. Crucially, the SSRC appealed to parents and workers to stay away from work and join their march to John Vorster Square, the police and security police HQ where many students were being detained and tortured. On 4 August, approximately 20,000 Sowetans marched along the Soweto Highway, the main road linking the township with the Johannesburg city centre. Considering the police's violent response to the march on 16 June, this was a remarkable demonstration of unity by students and parents to press home their demands. Unsurprisingly, the marchers were confronted by a cordon of police determined to stop them from reaching the city. If the students' demonstration in June had challenged the authority of the state in Soweto, this march had the potential of taking the struggle into the heartland of white South Africa. It was something the state was determined to prevent at all cost. Inevitably, a stand-off ensued, with the police firing live ammunition into the crowd of protesters. Three students were killed and many more were wounded, forcing a retreat back to the township.

In view of the short notice at which it was organised, the stayaway was successful, with an estimated 60 per cent of Soweto's workers heeding the call. Although the SSRC was popular among students, it had not yet established its credentials among large swathes of adults and workers. Nonetheless, many were sympathetic to the demands of the students and demonstrated their solidarity by joining the march. Others, however, were unable to go to work because students had disrupted the transport services. Buses and trains were stoned, and cars were stopped. Attempts by students to extend the stayaway by two more days failed, revealing tensions between themselves and workers, who were wary of losing wages and even their jobs. Despite these difficulties, the students proclaimed the action a victory. A pamphlet distributed after the strike asserted, 'We dealt the racist regime and factory-owners a heavy blow – they lost their profits.'

Emboldened by this success, the SSRC called for a second stayaway for 23 to 25 August. Unlike previously, the SSRC now had time to mobilise properly among students and parents. Sibongile Mkhabela explains how they went about it. 'The previous week had been spent in meetings with pupils in primary schools around Soweto. The strategy adopted by the SSRC involved talking to kids and asking them to appeal to their parents not to go to work on the 24th. Azikhwelwa, which is a call for a work stayaway, was our rallying cry. Frankly, I enjoyed the charged atmosphere and the discussions at the schools. The kids were curious and were asking interesting questions about politics, 16 June and the presence of armed patrols in our township and schools that had been there since 16 June.'

Students campaigned extensively in the township through door-to-door visits and the distribution of large numbers of leaflets. The response by students and workers was positive, reflected in the large numbers who joined the stayaway on the first day of *Azikhwelwa*. In an attempt to avoid further violent confrontations with the police, leaders of the movement decided not to plan any mass action on the day. This was by all accounts a successful demonstration of the SSRC's capacity to unite students and workers behind clear political demands and without intimidation. Most significantly, a reported 75 per cent of Johannesburg's African workforce was absent on 23 August. This was not only an improvement on the figures of the previous stayaway, but also represented the largest strike in Johannesburg since the early 1960s.

However, there was one major constituency that did not heed the call for a stayaway, namely, the hostel dwellers. Thousands of migrant workers, most of them single men, lived in dormitory-style hostels scattered across the township. They tended to be aloof from the townships and generally eschewed the urban lifestyle of these places. Few were interested in township politics, and they were even less inclined to accept instructions by young people to stay away from work. Moreover, there is little evidence to suggest that students made serious efforts to explain their campaign to the hostel dwellers. In fact, young activists perceived them mostly as strike-breakers. Groups of students therefore confronted hostel dwellers on their way back from work, which led to a violent confrontation. Two students were killed in the ensuing melee outside the Meadowlands hostel. An attempt to burn down this hostel, which housed close to 10,000 male migrants, caused tensions to rise sharply.

At this point the sinister hand of the state began to appear. Although there was no evidence of student involvement in the fire, the authorities quickly pointed an accusing finger at the SSRC. This was widely perceived by residents as an attempt by the state to drive a wedge between workers and students. More seriously, the police exploited the anger among sections of the hostel dwellers to organise violent attacks on Soweto residents. Evidence that the police, supported by the Urban Bantu Council (UBC), had fomented violence surfaced in the newspapers. One paper reported a UBC meeting where it was allegedly 'agreed that youngsters who stopped workers from going to work should be killed'. The most graphic details of police complicity came from a journalist who witnessed the Soweto police commander, General Gert Prinsloo, addressing hostel dwellers at Mzimhlope hostel. According to the journalist, Prinsloo handed out 'bread … packs of milk and mageu, so-called Bantu Beer' and told the inmates, 'Eat, so that when you kill you are full.' He then proceeded to issue them with clear instructions: 'You are warned not to continue to damage the houses because they belong to WRAB. If you damage houses, you will force us to take action against you to prevent this. You have been ordered to kill only the troublemakers.' A few weeks later, Gatsha Buthelezi (chief minister of the quasi-homeland of Zululand) castigated the police and declared he had no doubt that 'certain members of the police fanned these flames of anger between these black people'.

On the morning of 24 August a crowd of hostel dwellers

congregated at the Meadowlands hostel, armed with an assortment of 'traditional weapons', including sticks, assegais and knobkieries. From there they descended on Orlando West and Meadowlands, chanting, 'Where is your Black Power? Where is it?' Indiscriminate attacks on residents of the two areas followed, aimed at instilling maximum fear in the population. Patrick Hlongwe told the authors of *Soweto: A History* how he and his friends managed to evade the attackers: 'I hid inside the stove and closed the top and the wood blocked the stove. They went in and turned the house upside down and, when I met with my friends the next day, one told how he hid under the bed. Another said that he was in the roof. But in some other houses, they bashed down the ceiling. A lot of people were found in the roof and were killed.'

Many people packed their belongings and fled the township in panic. After recovering from the initial shock, township residents regrouped and fought back. They noticed immediately that the police would intervene on the side of the hostel dwellers, but stood by when the latter attacked them. A group of about 30 students from Orlando West planned petrol-bomb attacks against the hostels, seeking to shift the battle from the township to the hostels. Over the next few days Meadowlands and Orlando West resembled war zones, and at the end more than 30 people had been killed and over 350 injured. *The World* warned that 'anarchy is threatening to engulf townships in Soweto, with black fighting black residents'.

The violence also spread to other parts of Soweto, with sporadic pitched battles being fought between students and hostel dwellers over a period of two weeks. By early September the official death toll from this internecine conflict stood at 70.

Deep divisions and mutual suspicion between township residents and hostel dwellers appeared to be firmly entrenched. Certainly, the events of August 1976 presaged the violence that would periodically erupt between these groups over the next few decades, especially at moments of heightened struggle against apartheid. To counter the destructive consequences of this conflict, the SSRC, with the support of adult leaders, made serious efforts to overcome the existing divisions and build unity. For example, on 27 August the student body distributed a circular that aimed to make common cause with the hostel dwellers: 'The students have nothing against people living in the hostels, they are our parents, they are victims of the notorious migrant labour system. They are forced to live hundreds of miles away from their families, their needs and grievances are ignored by the powers that be. WE are aware that they are packed like sardines in small rooms with no privacy and living under appalling conditions. Yet when the students rise against these injustices and designers of our miserable lives, the powers that be suddenly realise that these are well meaning citizens. The puppet UBC, acting on instruction from Pretoria, deems it fit to arm our parents in the hostel against us. The students reject, *in toto*, the entire oppressive system with its largely pocket institutions like the UBC's and the Bantustans, those toy telephones are designed to divide the Black community. United we stand'.

Ten days later, on 7 September, the SSRC issued another circular addressed 'To all residents of Soweto, Hostels, Reef & Pretoria'. Recognising that the state's strategy was to use ethnicity to 'divide-and-rule' black people, it called for solidarity and warned township residents against 'false leaders':

1. Remember you are all blacks: Whether you are Zulu, Mosotho, Mopedi, Xosa, Motswana, Venda, etc. You are *one*: sons and daughters of the black cradle.
2. You will not kill your black brother, father, mother, son or daughter: Stop fighting among yourselves. Stop killing each other while the enemy is strong.
3. *Do not allow yourself to be divided*: Be united to face the common enemy: Apartheid, Exploitation and Oppression. Unity is strength! Solidarity is power!
4. *Beware of false leaders*: They will always run in the dark to Jimmy Kruger to sell out the true Sons and Daughters of the Black nations. They are tools and stooges of the oppressive system.

5. *Beware of Political Opportunists*: Who will always agitate Black people for their own end. They are cowards who cannot face the enemy by themselves. They want to use us. They will always spread false rumours in the name of the students.

6. *We say to all black students, residents and hostel inmates*: You know your true leaders. Listen to your leaders. Support your leaders. Follow your leaders.

This statement constituted part of a concerted effort to build unity among the different sectors of Soweto's population. It aimed particularly to involve hostel dwellers early and directly in plans for a third stayaway from 13 to 15 September. Another pamphlet appealed for solidarity, asking workers to co-operate with students and calling on hostel dwellers not to fight students. The shift in tactics yielded positive results and, in sharp contrast to the August events, migrant workers were active in mobilising support for the planned action. As a result, the stayaway was the most successful of the three strikes called by the SSRC. Buoyed by its accomplishments, the SSRC organised an audacious march in the heart of Johannesburg. Previous efforts to march from Soweto to the city had been violently stopped. Having learnt the lessons of those experiences, the SSRC adopted new tactics. On the morning of 23 September hundreds of students took various forms of public transport into the city and congregated in Eloff Street, one of Johannesburg's main retail thoroughfares. As they unfurled their banners and placards, the students were joined by workers, causing the assembled crowd to grow to about 1500. Their boldness elicited cries of support from black onlookers and panic among whites. As usual, the police arrived within minutes and forcibly dispersed the demonstrators. Although the *Azikhwelwa* campaign did not result in an end to state repression, it did generate considerable public attention. Its primary achievement was arguably to unite students and workers, in the face of considerable challenges. Moreover, it established a template for struggle that students elsewhere in the country began to seek to emulate.

Soweto everywhere

While Soweto was undoubtedly the centre of the student uprising, the issues raised by that movement affected black students across the country. Police violence against protesters in Soweto on 16 June prompted solidarity action by students in many townships throughout South Africa over the following days. They embraced the campaign against Afrikaans and, as in Soweto, they quickly began to mobilise against the apartheid system. On 17 and 18 June, Alexandra and some townships on the East Rand (now Ekurhuleni) became focal points of solidarity action. Thereafter, the movement spread to other parts of the country, to both rural and urban areas, and became especially intense in the Western Cape.

Students in Alexandra enjoyed close relations with their counterparts in Soweto, mainly because many of them attended schools in the bigger township. Some of them were members of SASM and were active in student politics in Soweto. When they returned home on the night of 16 June, these activists immediately set about organising the local students. Thato Sikhosana and others went around the township, informing students of a meeting that was planned for the following evening to discuss how the struggle could be taken up in Alexandra. At that meeting plans were formulated for a mass march through the township. Obed Bapela recalls what happened on the morning of 18 June at the only secondary school in the township, Alexandra Senior Secondary: 'Those who had addressed us went to the front and said, "no one goes to the classes". Some of us we stood and those who were trying to move from us you say hey, hey, hey stay, you say you stay because they didn't know what was happening. So we were all grounded and then they addressed us to say you have already seen what has happened in Soweto and what is happening in Soweto is affecting us also, Afrikaans as a medium of instruction is killing us, how do you do History in Afrikaans?'

In the meantime, other SASM activists were campaigning at the bus stops and taxi ranks for workers to join the solidarity march. As the students left Alexandra

Secondary School they were joined by several supporters. Following the example of Soweto, the march went from school to school. 'So we then went to Ithute which is just a primary school, singing there and the popular songs were "senzeni na!" [What have we done?] so as we were singing that song there were those who were going to Ithute small children, Standard 3, 4, 5, and they took them out and they say those who were still young please remain behind and they selected those who were older and then they joined the crowd. We then went down Selborne into 16th Avenue in that column, turned to the left to go to Bovedi, another primary school for the Tsongas and the Vendas. Then we went down 16th Avenue, came up 12th Avenue here and marched [along] 12th Avenue straight to Pholosho. We also selected those who were a bit older and then they joined the column, still police were not there and the crowd was growing and growing you know and then we sang "senzeni na!" and "thina si … lapha eAfrika!" [We are in Africa!] And that one we sang from 12th Avenue until Pholosho right at the top of 12th Avenue, "asoze si bulawa!" [We will not be killed!]'

As soon as the students embarked on their march, the police dispatched two platoons under the command of Colonel G. Slabbert to the township. From then until midnight Alexandra was engulfed in violence between the security forces and township students. It appeared as if the police were intent on taking revenge on the Alexandra youth for what had transpired in Soweto, and were particularly brutal in their attacks. In one incident in Selborne Street police opened fire on a group of 150, some of whom were looting a bottlestore, killing four and injuring several more. By the evening the violence had abated and there were only isolated incidents. The police admitted to shooting dead 29 people on 18 June, making it the most violent day until then in the township's history. A further five bodies were found in different parts of the township the following day. Selwyn Talaza, the son of an Anglican clergyman, and Japie Mankwe Vilankulu, an exponent of BC, were among those killed.

The first few days of the student uprising in Alexandra were characterised by the almost spontaneous involvement of hundreds of students. As in Soweto, students in Alexandra first attacked the obvious symbols of apartheid such as beerhalls and the West Rand Administration Board (WRAB) offices. Once the police force launched its assault on the township, the conflict rapidly intensified and resulted in numerous casualties and damage to properties. The demonstrations were remarkable for the unity displayed between African and coloured students, even though they attended segregated schools. But when some of the marchers turned their attention to looting shops in 1st Avenue, a more sinister side of the protest was exposed. This aspect of the demonstrations assumed racial overtones when Indian- and Chinese-owned shops were attacked and several were burned down. The intensity of the violence and especially the severity of the police reaction angered and shocked the community. Demonstrations and marches continued over the following weeks, though on a much smaller scale.

On 6 August PUTCO decided to withdraw its bus service from the township. Throughout this period regular attempts were made to burn down schools. The uprising in early August reached a climax on 9 August. The Cillie Commission later summarised the events on that day in its report as follows: 'Rioting was rife throughout the residential area. Buses and police vehicles were pelted with stones; rioters erected barricades in the streets, intimidation of workers was general.' Alexandra Secondary School and Kadide School were set on fire.

Alexandra activists found it more difficult to replicate the organisational successes of their Sowetan counterparts, mainly because there was only one secondary school in the area. Student leaders were unable to sustain the mobilisation of students and, when the SSRC called a three-day strike for 23 to 25 August, few workers from Alexandra heeded the call. Severe repression and organisational weaknesses had caused the uprising to run out of steam. On the first day of the September stayaway in Soweto, the state mounted a massive security operation to regain control over the township. According to *The World*, 'It is estimated that over 900 people in Alexandra were arrested yesterday in what police described as a "clean-up". The police launched a crackdown on children and adults found in the township during the day. They went from house to house looking for people not at work or school. The house-to-house search followed the stay-at-home strike in Soweto yesterday … A police spokesman said the massive arrests were intended to "clean up the township of loafers".

The security invasion of the township struck a heavy blow against the already weak student movement. As a result further attempts to mobilise support for a stayaway in October and for a boycott of the final school examinations enjoyed little success. Despite these setbacks, the struggle in Alexandra gave birth to a new generation of student and youth activists who, from early 1977, began to organise themselves in the Alexandra Students' League (ASL), which sought to emulate the role of the SSRC.

As news spread about the massive demonstration in Orlando and the police's brutal response on 16 June, students from townships in Ekurhuleni immediately began planning solidarity action. Several secondary schools organised demonstrations for the following day. On the morning of 17 June, students from Tembisa High marched to Boitumelong Senior Secondary with the aim of mobilising support for the solidarity action. Along the way, the column of marchers was confronted by the police. Then, as in townships across the country, the police intervened: 'We were disrupted. The police tear-gassed us and unleashed dogs on us. Students started running helter-skelter. We ran into a toilet. We got into a toilet, I'm sure we were about 15, if not 20 – in one toilet. It was easy to go in but when we had to get out we couldn't because we were pressing the door out.'

A familiar pattern of protest now unfolded in Tembisa. Large groups of students attacked what they perceived to be 'symbols of apartheid', such as bottlestores and beerhalls. By the time they reached their destination the number of marchers had swelled to approximately 2000. Part of the crowd smashed the windows of a store and tried to set it on fire. By midday, smaller groups of students broke away from the main march and began to attack other shops. In one incident a Portuguese-owned café at the Oakmoor railway station was attacked and the owner's vehicle set alight. Several shots were fired into the crowd, resulting in the death of four protesters. The Cillie Commission later reported that five persons were shot dead by the police.

As elsewhere, the character of the local protest movement changed rapidly. While the initial trigger of the uprising was opposition to Afrikaans, within a few days broader political demands were being made. Mike Figo Madlala, a student leader, recalls the shift that occurred: 'From the 18th the language changed from that we were going to approach Boitumelong to discuss Afrikaans as a medium of instruction and object against it. People were now talking about Bantu Education being a bad system. And as well they were talking about apartheid system.

You know, to say we are oppressed as a nation.'

At the same time the new leaders from both high schools began to organise themselves and, with the assistance of more experienced activists from Soweto and Alexandra, launched the Tembisa Students' Representative Council (TSRC) on 18 June. The objectives of the TSRC, according to Mike Madlala, were 'to take issues of students, their grievances to the principal. The body had to represent the aspirations of the students.' It was also pointed out that the TSRC 'shouldn't be highly political in spite of the fact that it was formed within the turmoil'. The state responded quickly to destroy the nascent student movement in Tembisa. On 21 June the security forces swooped on the township and arrested approximately 300 students and charged nearly 200 of them with public violence.

Other parts of Ekurhuleni experienced similar local uprisings. For example, on the evening of 17 June the Vosloorus community hall was set alight, apparently by protesting youth who had been marching through the township. PUTCO, the bus company that parked its vehicles in a depot adjacent to the hall, now took the precaution of moving its buses to the depot in Boksburg. This decision set in motion a chain of events the following day that saw Vosloorus momentarily explode. The following morning PUTCO drivers had to collect their buses from the town and then return to the township. Thousands of commuters were stranded and had to wait for nearly two hours before the first buses arrived at 5 am. The workers were incensed and began stoning the buses. PUTCO then decided to withdraw all the buses, effectively leaving the whole Vosloorus workforce stranded in the township. Apartheid planning had left the township without a railway connection, which made residents almost entirely dependent on the bus service. When 30,000 workers, including migrants residing in the large single-sex hostels, decided to stay at home rather than walk to their workplaces in Boksburg, the first stayaway began in Vosloorus. Workers, joined by students, gathered along MC Botha Avenue, the main road connecting the township to Boksburg, to demonstrate and show their solidarity with the students of Soweto. From there they proceeded to other parts of the township, attacking any building associated with the East Rand Administration Board or the government. In the space of four hours, the beerhall, the post office, the hostel office and the community hall were set ablaze or broken down by workers and students. The Vosloorus uprising was one of the first major demonstrations of worker and youth unity in action, and was significant also for the involvement of hostel dwellers.

On the morning of 18 June almost all school principals reported no obvious signs of trouble, except in Katlehong. The apparent quiet was soon shattered when secondary school students all over the East Rand gathered in mass meetings at their schools. From there they marched and demonstrated through the townships. Suddenly the authorities were confronted not just by isolated incidents in a single township, but by almost simultaneous protests across the entire region. The East Rand Administration Board (ERAB) immediately withdrew its personnel and effectively handed over the running of the townships to the police. The involvement of hostel dwellers in the June uprising in both Vosloorus and Katlehong was significant, especially considering the violence in Soweto in August. It showed that migrants were not opposed to the student movement and, in fact, might support the solidarity action undertaken. They were also shocked and outraged by the state's brutal repression of the student demonstrations. In the East Rand townships, hostel dwellers demonstrated with students against the use of Afrikaans and endorsed broader demands against apartheid.

In August and September large parts of the country experienced student demonstrations, boycotts and deadly confrontations with the police. By then, the Soweto uprising had evolved into a national rebellion by black youth. University students, mainly from black campuses but also supporters at white institutions, organised solidarity protests. Black Consciousness was widely embraced, as students rejected apartheid's racial labels and rallied behind the banner of black unity and power.

State repression escalates
September arguably marked the high point of the

uprising, in Soweto as well as nationally. Marches, boycotts, demonstrations, stayaways and conflict with the police reverberated in townships across the country. Such a concerted challenge to the apartheid state had not been witnessed since the late 1950s and the authorities were determined to crush it. The Minister of Justice, Jimmy Kruger, spelled out the government's approach in a speech to parliament. 'The black man knows his place,' he attempted to reassure his fellow white MPs, but then ominously warned, 'and if not, I'll show him his place.' State repression remained relentless throughout this period. Detentions were both indiscriminate and targeted particularly at the leadership of the SSRC and SASM. As early as July it was reported that dozens of Soweto students were being held in detention without being charged. That figure increased sharply during the latter half of the year. In early August, 140 Black Consciousness Movement activists were arrested countrywide in a crackdown designed to cripple the movement. Winnie Mandela, a key ally of the student movement, was banished to the small town of Brandfort in the Orange Free State. Other members of the BPA also came under attack both from the police and members of the UBC.

Soon after his election as chairman of the SSRC, Tsietsi Mashinini was declared public enemy number one by the state. An arrest warrant was issued and promises of a reward made to anyone who gave him up to the police. But he was able to evade arrest, being shielded by the community. In this way Mashinini was able to continue attending SSRC meetings, address public gatherings, mobilise in the community and issue pamphlets. However, he was permanently on the run. Eventually, the growing probability of detention and threats to his life forced him to flee the country. His successor, Sidney Khotso Seatlholo, initially did not face the same security threat, but this changed when the SSRC registered important successes in its campaigns. In January 1977 he was shot at by the police in an attempt on his life, and as a result he also went into exile. Dan Montsitsi then replaced him as the leader of the SSRC.

Sibongile Mkhabela's detention on 24 August exemplified the experiences of many leading activists: 'Well, I had known that the police were looking for me, but then the police were looking for anybody and everybody in the township. I was shocked to realise how desperate they were to put me behind bars. I knew then I was in serious trouble. It had been a very long and painful day. The 14-hour interrogation had consisted of being kicked and slapped around by six well-built White policemen. I felt so tired, numb, and listless and only wanting a place to lay my head and rest … I was detained under the notorious Section 6 of the Terrorism Act, which gave power to the State to indefinitely detain anybody without trial.' She was only released in January 1977. Many others, including key figures like Seth Mazibuko, were detained and put on trial. In Ekurhuleni, the police acted swiftly to undermine the burgeoning student movement and arrested scores of students. Some of them faced charges ranging from sabotage to distributing pamphlets. In November, 13 Katlehong students appeared in court on charges of sabotage. They were accused of inciting other students from Katlehong Secondary School to march to the police station to demand the release of students. In what was probably the biggest trial in the region, 57 people from Katlehong and Daveyton were charged with public violence in the Germiston regional court. By October 1976 more than 1200 people had been convicted on a range of offences, including public violence, riotous assembly and arson.

Confronted by this massive security crackdown, an increasing number of students and youth decided to leave the country. Intense debates took place among activists about the merits of going into exile and of joining the armed struggle. Echoing a perennial debate in the liberation movement, many argued that the priority was to build a mass internal movement. For others, the most appropriate response to the state's violence was to join the military wings of the ANC and PAC. Prior to the uprising only a handful of activists had linked up with the external liberation organisations. But from the latter part of 1976 the trickle of students leaving to join their ranks turned into a steady stream. More than 600 Africans students and close to 300 adults are thought to have gone into exile in 1976 alone. The ANC and its military wing, Umkhonto weSizwe, were the principal beneficiaries of this development. This was reflected in the changes in the ANC's political messages. Immediately after the June uprising, ANC pamphlets called on 'people in every walk of life – in the factories, townships, mines, schools, farms, to embark on massive protests, actions and demonstrations against white supremacy'. Here the emphasis was on mass mobilisation based on the unity of the workers and youth. On 16 December, the anniversary of the founding of Umkhonto weSizwe, the ANC repeated its belief 'that only through armed struggle … could freedom be won'. To this end, it appealed to 'our youth – African, Indian and Coloured, [to] join Umkhonto in even bigger numbers and train to become skilled freedom fighters'.

Such appeals were received enthusiastically among sections of the youth. But the departure of so many young and committed activists, together with mass detentions, weakened the internal mass movements, especially the SSRC and SASM. It proved difficult to replace charismatic and politically astute activists such as Mashinini, Mkhabela, Mazibuko and others who had played formative roles in shaping the student movement. In the circumstances, the sheer survival of activists and their organisations was in fact a major accomplishment.

Rebellion winds down

Following the intense activities of August and September

the movement began to decline. Schools remained mostly abandoned, the open warfare on the streets had more or less come to halt by October, and further efforts to organise stayaways and marches generated little support. The SSRC retained enormous influence in Soweto and also garnered support across the country as other student movements looked to it for leadership. It used this authority to appeal to oppressed people nationally to observe 1976 as a 'Year of Mourning'. Recognising the enormous sacrifices made during the uprising, the SSRC called on people to suspend the usual festivities over the Christmas period, 'for the sake of our kids who died from police bullets'. It appealed to the community not to buy presents, hold parties or drink at shebeens. Consumption of liquor was a particularly important target for the students. 'Our daily experience', wrote the SSRC, 'is that nothing good has ever come out of shebeens. Many of our black sisters have been raped and/or murdered by drunkards and thugs from shebeens. Shebeens have become houses of vice and immorality. We cannot tolerate to see our fathers' pay packets being emptied into shebeens … Shebeens must close down.' These appeals enjoyed widespread support as Sowetans reflected on how their lives had been completely transformed by the eruption of the student protests.

The SSRC's primary focus in November was to organise a boycott of the end-of-year examinations. Little schooling had taken place since June, and few students were prepared to sit for the final examinations.

But there were also mixed feelings among some parents and students about the prospect of losing an entire year of education and thus having to repeat grades. Most, however, felt this was a sacrifice worth making. The BPA, which had previously called on students to return to school, also supported the boycott because it believed that normal schooling could only resume when detentions had stopped. As a result, the boycott enjoyed unanimous support. A similar position was adopted in other parts of the country, especially in the Cape, where the boycott was almost 100 per cent effective. Initially, the state responded by issuing standard threats but it quickly recognised that it did not have the power to force students to write the examinations. It therefore made plans for supplementary examinations to be taken in March 1977.

To all Form III students. Urgent Call.

1. From Monday 8th October, 1976

2. Instructions:

    a) Go back to school on Monday and write your examinations because it is your only chance – Matrics and others will get another chance in 1977 before March. *The sacrifices you have brought for Azania will bear fruit. You can only free yourself from the shackles of the oppressor if you are educated. Time is running out!!!*

    b) *Parents*: Send your children to write the exams otherwise you should have paid money for nothing.

c) *Tsotsis and others*: Please do not disturb those who want to write.

d) *Teachers and Principals*: Please be on duty and stop fooling.

e) *Shopkeepers*: Thank you for responding to our call – you may go back to normal trading hours now.

When the schools reopened in January 1977, the SSRC again had to face the contentious question of whether to support a continuation of the school boycott. Further complicating the issue was the government's proposal for supplementary examinations to take place in March. Opinions were sharply divided and the SSRC found it increasingly difficult to manage internal political divisions, which diminished its capacity to provide decisive leadership. Distinct factions emerged at an SSRC meeting held at Naledi High where 'tempers were high'. Sibongile Mkhabela was strongly opposed to writing the examinations. 'Some of us were simmering with anger,' she recalls, and she felt that 'if we continued with examinations we would be selling out on our comrades in jail'. She explains further: 'I could not understand how I could sit for the examinations whilst a significant number of students and Black leaders were languishing in our prisons. I felt this would be the worst betrayal of our struggle and our comrades. I agonised about this matter and my anger knew no bounds. How could we even contemplate the normal when the 10th floor of John Vorster Square continued to destroy Black lives with impunity?'

However, other students argued that education was important, not only for the advancement of individuals, but also for the struggle. For them, 'continued education was not negotiable'. Cognisant of the danger posed by the issue to the unity of the SSRC, it was decided not to impose a particular decision on all students. Instead, individual students were left to decide. Mkhabela recalls that the main consideration of the meeting was to maintain the unity of the SSRC: 'The SSRC and students finally reached a compromise, and the least polarised and confrontational decision was made. The student leaders could not compromise the unity of the students. The decision taken emphasised this need. Student leaders also felt that their role was not to defeat or alienate a section of the student body, but to provide direction.'

Many students were extremely unhappy about this course of action and accused the SSRC of failing to provide leadership. But parents were generally strongly in favour of a resumption of teaching, notwithstanding their sympathy for the students' cause. By February most students had returned to school and many chose to sit for the supplementary examinations. Relative calm prevailed at most schools, though beneath the surface of the apparent return to normality deep anger and resentment persisted. The extreme violence of the preceding months remained fresh in students' minds. They were traumatised and found it difficult to settle back into a 'normal routine'. Schools were crisis-ridden, the loss of one year's education was compounded by overcrowding, school governing structures were in disarray, and teaching facilities remained in a parlous state.

Afrikaans may have been withdrawn, but the apartheid government was still resolutely committed to the system of Bantu Education, which was a vital cog in its machinery of racial oppression. It misunderstood or chose to ignore the deep resentment towards the education system imposed on black people and Africans in particular. Students may have been in the forefront of the struggle but many teachers and parents also abhorred the system. During the course of 1977, half of Soweto's 19 school boards and 600 teachers resigned in protest against Bantu Education. Thamsanqa Kambule, the renowned educator and principal of Orlando High for 20 years, spoke for many when he said that his conscience had forced him to resign.

Overall, the student movement had been in decline since September 1976 and by early 1977 there were few signs of mass mobilisation. But the state was unable to regain the hegemony it had enjoyed prior to the June uprising. Its infrastructure of control in the townships, such as the network of Administration Board offices and beerhalls, lay in ruins. Its political allies in the Urban

Bantu Councils and on the school boards were utterly discredited. As a result, the apartheid state's presence in Soweto and other townships had been stripped down to its bare essence – armed bodies of men. But students and youth had already demonstrated that, despite the state's monopoly over firepower, they were prepared to confront the security forces.

Throughout the period of the uprising, the state's primary response was one of brutal repression. Its aim was quite simply to crush and eliminate any form of dissent and, as Jimmy Kruger so chillingly warned, to put black people in their place. Killings, detentions, harassment and trials continued even when the student movement and its main organisations – the SSRC and SASM – experienced decline. The state also moved decisively to silence the Black Consciousness Movement. The murder of Black Consciousness founder and leader, Steve Biko, in September 1977 was indicative of the extent to which the state would go to destroy its opponents. After months of ongoing repression, the SSRC was also finally banned in October 1977.

These were devastating blows against the student organisations and Black Consciousness more broadly. Within a year it appeared that the government had smashed the emerging anti-apartheid movement, much as it had done in the early 1960s. However, the setbacks experienced in 1977 proved to be temporary. The Soweto uprising of 1976, together with the Durban strikes of

1973, had rejuvenated the primary forces of the liberation movement, namely black workers and youth. What the momentous events of 1976 demonstrated was the capacity of young black people to overcome the shackles imposed by apartheid and collectively create a new political movement. From this moment on, black youth would play a pivotal role in shaping the character of the struggle against apartheid.

In the aftermath of the Soweto uprising the state responded by tentatively moving towards the adoption of a reform strategy. It established the Riekert and Wiehahn commissions to consider the right of Africans to be regarded as permanent residents in 'white cities' and the legal status of African workers (and thus their right to join trade unions), respectively. Urban Bantu Councils were abandoned and replaced, first, with Community Councils and, thereafter, with Black Local Authorities. In recognition of the deepening housing crisis, a new programme of housing construction was initiated. None of these reform measures addressed the underlying problems of apartheid and were rejected by the majority of black people as wholly inadequate. By the early 1980s many of the problems that had begun to manifest themselves a decade before, such as unemployment, shortage of houses, poor schooling and deteriorating conditions in townships, had in fact worsened.

Consequently, a new wave of rebellion swept across the country. Once again, students and youth were central actors in what became the most decisive movement against apartheid. Its high point was the unity achieved between students and workers, exemplified by the stayaway of 5–6 November 1984. Undoubtedly, the historic Soweto student uprising of 1976 not only inspired subsequent rebellions but also played a crucial role in producing a template for contentious politics that would be emulated in the 1980s and beyond.

Select bibliography

P. Bonner and N. Nieftagodien, *Alexandra: A History*, Johannesburg, Wits University Press, 2008

P. Bonner and N. Nieftagodien, *Ekurhuleni: The Making of an Urban Region*, Johannesburg, Wits University Press, 2012

P. Bonner and N. Nieftagodien, *Kathorus: A History*, Cape Town, Maskew Miller Longman, 2001

P. Bonner and L. Segal, *Soweto: A History*, Cape Town, Maskew Miller Longman, 1998

E. Brink, Steve Lebelo, Sue Krige and Dumisane Ntshangase, *Soweto 16 June 1976: Personal Accounts of the Uprising*, Cape Town, Kwela Books, 2006

P.M. Cillie, *Report of the Commission of Inquiry into the Riots at Soweto and Elsewhere from 16th June to the 28th February 1977*, Pretoria, Government Printer, 1977

N.J. Diseko, 'The Origins and Development of the South African Students' Movement, SASM: 1968–1976', *Journal of Southern African Studies*, 18/1, 1991

G.M. Gerhart, *Black Power in South Africa: The Evolution of an Ideology*, Berkeley, University of California Press, 1978

C. Glaser, *Bo-tsotsi: The Youth Gangs of Soweto, 1935–1976*, London, James Currey, 2000

B. Hirson, *Year of Fire, Year of Ash. The Soweto Revolt: Roots of a Revolution*, London, Zed Press, 1979

A.K. Hlongwane (ed.), *Footprints of the 'Class of 76': Commemoration, Memory, Mapping and Heritage*, Johannesburg, Hector Pieterson Memorial and Museum, 2008

J. Hyslop, *The Classroom Struggle: Policy and Resistance in South Africa, 1940–1990*, Pietermaritzburg, University of Natal Press, 1990

J. Kane-Berman, *Soweto: Black Revolt, White Reaction*, Johannesburg, Ravan Press, 1978

T. Lodge, *Black Politics in South Africa since 1945*, Johannesburg, Ravan Press, 1983

H. Mashabela, *A People on the Boil: Reflections on June 16 1976 and Beyond*, Johannesburg, Jacana Media, 2006

S. Mkhabela, *Open Earth and Black Roses: Remembering 16 June 1976*, Johannesburg, Skotaville Press, 2001

T. Moloi, 'Youth Politics: The Political Role of AZANYU in the Struggle for Liberation: The Case of AZANYU Thembisa branch, 1980s to 1996', MA research report, University of the Witwatersrand, 2006

P. Morris, *A History of Black Housing in South Africa*, Johannesburg, South African Foundation, 1980

S. Ndlovu, *The Soweto Uprising: Counter-Memories of June 1976*, Johannesburg, Ravan Press, 1998

S. Ndlovu, N. Nieftagodien and T. Moloi, 'The Soweto Uprising', in *The Road to Democracy in South Africa, Volume 2 [1970–1980]*, Pretoria, Unisa Press, 2006

N. Nieftagodien, 'The Township Uprising, September–November 1984', in *Turning Points in History: People, Places and Apartheid*, No. 5, Johannesburg, STE Publishers, 2004

N. Nieftagodien and S. Gaule, *Orlando West, Soweto: An Illustrated History*, Johannesburg, Wits University Press, 2012

D. O'Meara, *Forty Lost Years: The Apartheid State and the Politics of the National Party, 1948–1994*, Johannesburg, Ravan Press, 1996

H. Pohlandt-McCormick, "'I Saw a Nightmare …" Doing Violence to Memory: The Soweto Uprising, June 16, 1976', PhD thesis, University of Minnesota, 1999

D. Posel, *The Making of Apartheid, 1948–1961: Conflict and Compromise*, Oxford, Clarendon Press, 1991

Acknowledgements

I would like to thank Wits University Press for granting me permission to reproduce sections from the following books: P. Bonner and N. Nieftagodien, *Alexandra: A History* (Wits University Press, 2008); P. Bonner and N. Nieftagodien, *Ekurhuleni: The Making of an Urban Region* (Wits University Press, 2012); and N. Nieftagodien and S. Gaule, *Orlando West, Soweto: An Illustrated History* (Wits University Press, 2012).

My colleagues in the Historical and Literary Papers department at the University of the Witwatersrand Library were once again extremely helpful in accessing photographs. Penelope Makghati and Élan Nieftagodien provided important research assistance, while Zahn Gowar lent her professional hand to various administrative matters, including the index. Shariefa Allie-Nieftagodien's constant support is largely responsible for the book being completed.

Index

Printed in the USA
CPSIA information can be obtained
at www.ICGtesting.com
LVHW061939150823
755329LV00005B/244